First World War
and Army of Occupation
War Diary
France, Belgium and Germany

51 DIVISION
Divisional Troops
Divisional Signal Company
1 May 1915 - 27 February 1919

WO95/2856/2

The Naval & Military Press Ltd
www.nmarchive.com
Published in association with The National Archives

Published by

The Naval & Military Press Ltd

Unit 10 Ridgewood Industrial Park,

Uckfield, East Sussex,

TN22 5QE England

Tel: +44 (0) 1825 749494

www.naval-military-press.com

www.nmarchive.com

This diary has been reprinted in facsimile from the original. Any imperfections are inevitably reproduced and the quality may fall short of modern type and cartographic standards.

© **Crown Copyright**
Images reproduced by permission of The National Archives, London, England, 2015.

Contents

Document type	Place/Title	Date From	Date To
Heading	WO95/2856/2 51st Divisional Signal Company May 1915-Mar 1919		
Heading	51st Division 51st Divl Signal Coy RE. May 1915-Mar 1919		
Heading	51st Signal Coy RE Vol I May-July		
War Diary	Field Stn YEA	01/05/1915	30/07/1915
Heading	51st Division 51st Signal Coy RE Vol II August 15		
War Diary	Field	01/08/1915	31/08/1915
Heading	51st Division 51st Divl Signal Coy RE Vol III September 1915		
War Diary	Field	01/09/1915	30/09/1915
War Diary	51st Division 51st Signal Coy RE Vol IV Oct 15		
War Diary	Field	01/10/1915	31/10/1915
Heading	51st Div Signal Coy Nov 1915 Vol V		
War Diary	Field	01/11/1915	30/11/1915
Map	51st Highland Divisional Signal Company		
Heading	51st Divl Signal Co. RE Dec Vol VI		
War Diary		01/12/1915	31/12/1915
Diagram etc	Diagram		
Heading	Signal Coy Vol 7.8.9. & 10		
War Diary	Field	02/01/1916	22/04/1916
Heading	War Diary Of The 51st (Highland) Divn Signal Coy R.E.T. From 1st May-31st May 1916		
War Diary	Hermaville	01/05/1916	31/05/1916
Heading	War Diary Of The 51st (Highland) Divn Signal Coy R.E.T. From 1st June To 30th June 1916		
War Diary	Hermaville	01/06/1916	30/06/1916
Heading	War Diaries Of The 51st (Highland) Divn Signal Coy R.E.T From 1st July To 31st July 1916		
War Diary	Hermaville	01/07/1916	14/07/1916
War Diary	Villers Chatel	14/07/1916	14/07/1916
War Diary	Doullens	15/07/1916	15/07/1916
War Diary	Ribeaucourt Dept Somme	16/07/1916	19/07/1916
War Diary	Ribemont	20/07/1916	21/07/1916
War Diary	Fricourt	21/07/1916	27/07/1916
Heading	51st Divisional Engineers 51st (Highland) Divisional Signal Company R.E August 1916		
War Diary	Field	01/08/1916	31/08/1916
Heading	War Diary For 51st (High) Divisional Signal Co R.E. (T) For September 1916		
War Diary	Field	01/09/1916	22/09/1916
War Diary	Stenwerk	22/09/1916	30/09/1916
War Diary	Beauval	01/10/1916	01/10/1916
War Diary	Bus	02/10/1916	21/10/1916
Heading	War Diary 51st (H) Divl. Signal Co. 1st November To 30 November 1916 Vol 25		
War Diary	Lealvillers	01/11/1916	30/11/1916
Diagram etc	51st Divn. Signals-Circuit Diagram		
Heading	War Diary Of 51st (Highland) Divisional Signal Co From 1st December 1916 To 31st December 1916		

War Diary	Usna	01/12/1916	31/12/1916
Heading	War Diary 51st (Highland) Divisional Signal Co. From 1st January 1917 To 31st January 1917.		
War Diary	Usna Hill	01/01/1917	16/01/1917
War Diary	Burgny	17/01/1917	31/01/1917
Miscellaneous	51st Divisional Signal School		
Heading	War Diary Of 51st (Highland) Divisional Signal Co., R.E. From 1st February, 1917 To 28th February, 1917.		
War Diary	Buigny St Maclou	01/02/1917	28/02/1917
Heading	War Diary For 51st (H) Divisional Signal Co. R.E. From 1st To 31st March 1917 Vol 21		
Heading	51st (H) Divisional Signal Co.R.E (T) March 1917		
War Diary	Villers Chatel	01/03/1917	31/03/1917
Heading	War Diary April 1917 51st (Highland) Signal Co. R.E (T) Vol 22		
War Diary	Field	01/04/1917	30/04/1917
Heading	War Diary For May 1917 51st (H) Divisional Signal Co. R.E (T) Vol 23		
War Diary		01/05/1917	31/05/1917
Heading	War Diary June 1917 51st (H) Divnl Signal Co. R.E (T) Vol 24		
War Diary		04/06/1917	22/06/1917
War Diary	Field	01/06/1917	30/06/1917
Heading	War Diary July 1917 51st (H) Divnl Sig Co. R.E (T) Vol 25		
War Diary	Field	01/07/1917	31/07/1917
Heading	War Diary Of 51st (Highland) Divisional Signal Company RE. T.F From 1st August 1917 To 31st August 1917		
War Diary	Camp	01/08/1917	23/08/1917
War Diary	Wormhout	23/08/1917	28/08/1917
War Diary	Border Camp	29/08/1917	31/08/1917
Miscellaneous	51st Divisional Signals	27/08/1917	27/08/1917
Heading	War Diary of 51st (Highland) Signal Company RE T.F. from 1st Septbr 1917 to 30th Septbr 1917		
War Diary	Border Camp	01/09/1917	25/09/1917
War Diary	Wormhout	26/09/1917	29/09/1917
War Diary	Achiet Le Petit	30/09/1917	30/09/1917
Miscellaneous			
Miscellaneous	XVIII Corps No. G.S. 66/252	16/10/1917	16/10/1917
Miscellaneous	51st (Highland) Divisional Signal Company	28/09/1917	28/09/1917
Diagram etc	Trunk Telephone Communications		
Diagram etc	Scheme Of Brigade Communication		
Heading	War Diary October 1917 51st (H) Signal Co. R.E (T) Vol 28		
War Diary	Boisleux Au Mont	01/10/1917	31/10/1917
Diagram etc	51st Highland Division		
Heading	51st Divisional Engineers 51st Divisional Signal Company R.E November 1917		
Heading	51D Signals Vol 29 War Diary November 1917 51st (H) Divisional Signal Co. R.E (T)		
War Diary	Boisleux	01/11/1917	01/11/1917
War Diary	Hermaville	02/11/1917	16/11/1917
War Diary	Little Wood Ytres	17/11/1917	19/11/1917
War Diary	Ytres	19/11/1917	21/11/1917
War Diary	Trescault	21/11/1917	23/11/1917

War Diary	Flesquieres	23/11/1917	24/11/1917
War Diary	Baizieux	25/11/1917	30/11/1917
Miscellaneous	51st (H) Division	05/12/1917	05/12/1917
Miscellaneous	51st (H) Divisional Signal Co R.E (T)	30/11/1917	30/11/1917
Diagram etc	51st (Highland) Divisional Signal Coy R.E T.F.		
Miscellaneous	CRA		
Heading	51st D Signals Vol 30 War Diary For December 1917 51st (H) Divl Sig. Co R.E. (T)		
War Diary	Lechelle	01/12/1917	01/12/1917
War Diary	Ytres	01/12/1917	02/12/1917
War Diary	Fremicourt	03/12/1917	30/12/1917
Heading	War Diary For January 1918 51st (H) Divnl Signal Co. R.E (T) Vol 31		
War Diary	Fremicourt	01/01/1918	20/01/1918
War Diary	Achiet Le Petit	21/01/1918	31/01/1918
Heading	51 D Signal Vol 32 War Diary February 1918 51st (H) Divnl Signal Co. R.E (T)		
War Diary	Achiet Le Petit	01/02/1918	11/02/1918
War Diary	Fremicourt	13/02/1918	28/02/1918
Heading	51st Divisional Engineers War Diary 51st Signal Company R.E March 1918		
Heading	War Diary 51st (H) Div. Sig Co. RE March 1918 Vol 33		
War Diary	Fremicourt	01/03/1918	27/03/1918
War Diary	Souastre	28/03/1918	31/03/1918
Heading	51st Divisional Engineers War Diary 51st Divisional Signal Company R.E April 1918		
War Diary	Fouqueres	01/04/1918	04/04/1918
War Diary	Labreuvriere	05/04/1918	07/04/1918
War Diary	Robecq	08/04/1918	12/04/1918
War Diary	Busnes	12/04/1918	14/04/1918
War Diary	Lambres	15/04/1918	19/04/1918
War Diary	Norrent Fontes	20/04/1918	30/04/1918
Miscellaneous	51st (H) Divisional Signal Coy. R.E (T) Report On Communication.	28/04/1918	28/04/1918
Miscellaneous	51st Division G	28/04/1918	28/04/1918
Diagram etc	Diagram		
Heading	War Diary Of 51st (H) Div. Signal Co. R.E For May 1918		
War Diary	Norrent Fontes	01/05/1918	05/05/1918
War Diary	Maroeuil	06/05/1918	31/05/1918
Heading	War Diary Of 51st (H) Div. Signal Co. RE For June 1918 Vol 36		
Heading	War Diary June 1918 51st High. Divnl. Signal Coy R.E T.F.		
War Diary	Maroeuil	01/06/1918	30/06/1918
Heading	Divisional Engineers, 51st (Highland) Division. 51st Divisional Signal Co. R.E. July 1918		
Heading	War Diary Of 51st (H) Div. Signal Co. R.E T.F For July 1918 Vol 37		
War Diary	Maroeuil	01/07/1918	10/07/1918
War Diary	Rollecourt	11/07/1918	14/07/1918
War Diary	Nogent-N-Seine	15/07/1918	15/07/1918
War Diary	Villenauxe	16/07/1918	16/07/1918
War Diary	St. Prix	17/07/1918	17/07/1918
War Diary	Moussy	18/07/1918	18/07/1918

War Diary	Hautevillers	19/07/1918	19/07/1918
War Diary	St. Imoges	20/07/1918	22/07/1918
War Diary	Hautevillers	23/07/1918	27/07/1918
War Diary	Nanteuil.	27/07/1918	30/07/1918
War Diary	Cramont	31/07/1918	31/07/1918
Miscellaneous	'G' 51st (H) Division	10/08/1918	10/08/1918
Miscellaneous	51st (H) Divisional Signal Coy. R.E. (T).	10/08/1918	10/08/1918
Heading	War Diary 51st (High) Divisional Signal Coy RE T.F. For August 1918 Vol 38		
War Diary	Cramont	01/08/1918	03/08/1918
War Diary	Villers-Chatel	04/08/1918	15/08/1918
War Diary	Maroeuil	16/08/1918	31/08/1918
Miscellaneous	51st (H) Divisional Signal Coy R.E (T)	10/08/1918	10/08/1918
Heading	War Diary Of 51st (H) Div. Signal Co. R.E. T.F. For September 1918 Vol 39		
War Diary	Victory Camp North Of Arras	01/09/1918	13/09/1918
War Diary	Maroeuil	14/09/1918	25/09/1918
War Diary	Victory Camp	26/09/1918	30/09/1918
Heading	War Diary 51st (H) Divisional Signal Coy. October 1918 Vol 40		
Heading	War Diary 51st Divisional Signal Coy		
War Diary	Victory Camp	01/10/1918	03/10/1918
War Diary	Chateau D'Acq	04/10/1918	07/10/1918
War Diary	Inchy En Artois	08/10/1918	09/10/1918
War Diary	Bourlon	10/10/1918	10/10/1918
War Diary	Escadoeuvres	11/10/1918	11/10/1918
War Diary	Naves	12/10/1918	20/10/1918
War Diary	Avesnes Le Sec	20/10/1918	28/10/1918
War Diary	Basse Ville De Bouchain	29/10/1918	30/10/1918
War Diary	Iwuy	31/10/1918	31/10/1918
Diagram etc	Avesnes-Le-Sec		
Diagram etc	Diagram		
Miscellaneous	51st (H) Divisional Signal Coy. R.E. (T).	03/11/1918	03/11/1918
Miscellaneous	S.G.745/97	01/11/1918	01/11/1918
Miscellaneous	51st (H) Divisional Signal Coy. R.E. (T).	03/11/1918	03/11/1918
Heading	War Diary Of 51st (H) Div. Signal Co. RE. From 1st To 30th November 1918 Vol 41		
War Diary	Iwuy	01/11/1918	30/11/1918
Heading	War Diary Of 51st (H) Div. Signal Co. R.E. For December 1918 Vol 42		
War Diary	Iwuy	01/12/1918	31/12/1918
War Diary	Iwuy	01/01/1919	07/01/1919
War Diary	Houdeng	07/01/1919	24/01/1919
War Diary	Houdeng Goegnies	27/02/1919	27/02/1919

WO 95/2856/2

51st Divisional Signal Company

MAY 1915 - MAR 1919

51 ST DIVISION

51ST DIVL SIGNAL COY RE.

MAY 1915-MAR 1919

121/6390.

51st Division

61st Signal Coy RE

Vol I. May–July

WAR DIARY or INTELLIGENCE SUMMARY

(Erase heading not required.)

Army Form C. 2118.

For month ending 31st May, 1915.

51st Highld Divnl Signal Co

Place	Date	Hour	Summary of Events and Information	Remarks and references to Appendices
Field Stn U.S.A.	MAY. 1st to 3rd.		Headquarters and number 1 section 51st Highland Divisional Signal Co left Bedford at 6.30 am on 30th April arriving at Southampton about 1 pm and sailed by troopship S.S. City of Lucknow at 4.30 pm. Two Torpedo boats acted as escorts. Communication by means of electric signalling lamp was kept up all night with the destroyers by the Coy. Nos 2, 3 & 4 sections travelled to France with their own Infantry Brigades. Headqrs and number 1 section disembarked at Havre at 10 am on 1st May. Left Havre by train at 10.55 pm and arrived at Berguette about 6 pm on 2nd May. Headquarters of Division at Chateau Buaves being reached about 10 pm same date. Communication with Indian Corps had been opened two days before arrival.	
	4th		Cable lines were laid between Brigade Headqrs & Divl Headqrs; 152nd Infantry Brigade–Robecq; 153rd Inf Bde – Lillers then Paradis; 154th Inf Bde – Ham then Calonne.	
	5th to 13th		Excellent communication was maintained between Brigade Headquarters and Divisional Headquarters.	

WAR DIARY for month ending May 31/4/15. Army Form C. 2118.

or

INTELLIGENCE SUMMARY. 51st (Highld) Divl Signal Co.

(Erase heading not required.)

Instructions regarding War Diaries and Intelligence Summaries are contained in F.S. Regs., Part II. and the Staff Manual respectively. Title pages will be prepared in manuscript.

Place	Date	Hour	Summary of Events and Information	Remarks and references to Appendices
	MAY.			
Field Sn. USA	14th		On Division being ordered to proceed to Pradelle Coy left Busnes at 10 am and arrived Chateau Pradelle about 4 pm	
	15th		Communication was opened between Brigade Headqrs and Divl Headqrs, also to General Headqrs Report Centre & 3rd Corps Headqrs. 152nd. Strazeel. 153rd. Caestre 154th. Meteren	
	16th & 17th		Communication between Brigade Headqrs & Divisional Headqrs was well maintained	
	18th 19th		Left Pradelle at 7 pm and arrived at Lapogue about 1 am. As an advanced Headqrs was opened at La Couture two cable detachments were sent there and arrived about 4 pm. Staff left at Lapogue to deal with "Administrative work. While detachments were entering La Couture village was heavily shelled.	
	20th		Relieved 2nd Divisional Signal Co taking over their system of communication between Divisional Headqrs and Bde Headqrs. Communication to Indian Corps was also taken over.	

WAR DIARY or INTELLIGENCE SUMMARY

Army Form C. 2118.

WAR DIARY for month ending 31st May 1915.
INTELLIGENCE SUMMARY. 51st (Highld) Divl Signal Coy

Place	Date	Hour	Summary of Events and Information	Remarks and references to Appendices
Field Sta. Y9A	MAY. 20th		152nd Infantry Brigade Near Locon	
			153rd Infantry Brigade Richebourg St. Vaast	
			154th Infantry Brigade Le Hamel.	
	21st to		L/Cpl. J. Scholls 51st (Highld) Divl Signal Co. wounded in leg by shrapnel. Two cable sections left at Indelle went to Locon and opened office there to deal with Administrative work.	
	25th		Communication to Brigade Headqrs was very often interrupted though shell fire, but was quickly restored — no inconvenience being caused. 369 L/Cpl G. Forbes, 480 Pnr. G. Easton, 812 Pnr. S. Macaulay of 51st (Highld) Divl Sig. Co were wounded by shrapnel on 22nd May.	
	26th		As the village of Labouture had been heavily shelled for the last two or three days it was thought advisable to shift the other two cable detachments to Locon, Company headquarters personnel being left to deal with General Staff work.	
	27th		Locoture was heavily shelled with high explosives from early morning	

WAR DIARY for month ending 31st May 1915

Army Form C. 2118.

INTELLIGENCE SUMMARY. 51st (Highld) Divsl Signal Co.

(Erase heading not required.)

Instructions regarding War Diaries and Intelligence Summaries are contained in F.S. Regs, Part II. and the Staff Manual respectively. Title pages will be prepared in manuscript.

Place	Date	Hour	Summary of Events and Information	Remarks and references to Appendices
Field nr Ypres	27th		Communication with Brigade Headquarters frequently interrupted but quickly restored. At 12 noon high explosives were landing every minute round about chateau Headquarters was situated in. Orders were issued by "General Staff" to Major Robertson that headqrs personnel of 51st Highld Divsl Signal Co were to proceed two or three hundred yards down road towards Vieille Chapelle while doing so a shell landed in midst of party killing two (615 a4pr. 103 Fulgoun 51st (Highld) Divsl Sygnal Co) and wounding two (603 Corpl C B Ireland 51st (Highld) Divl Bycleist Co) and Pte J M Alexander & 512 Qmr J.S. Murray of 51st (Highld) Divl Sig Co). J S Murray subsequently dying. On attempting to resume work in office shelling became so violent that General Staff issued orders to remove office to Locon which was accordingly done the same night. Everything quiet communications maintained	
	28th & 29th 30th		Duncan transferred to 4th Corps & communication established to Hq.Co.	

WAR DIARY *for month ending 31st May 1915* **or INTELLIGENCE SUMMARY.** 51st (Highd) Divl Signal Co

(Erase heading not required.)

Place	Date	Hour	Summary of Events and Information	Remarks and references to Appendices
	MAY.			
Field Staff	31st		Communication maintained with Brigade Headquarters 152nd Inf. Bde Moat Farm 153rd " Le Touret. 154th " Hinges. During May the lines were patrolled carefully every day.	

WAR DIARY for month ending 30th June 1915.

Army Form C. 2118.

INTELLIGENCE SUMMARY. 51st (Highd) Divl Signal Co

(Erase heading not required.)

Place	Date	Hour	Summary of Events and Information	Remarks and references to Appendices
Field Sig. Coy	JUNE 1st.		Mr Asquith passed through Locon inspecting Highd Division.	
	2nd.		Communication maintained	
	3rd.		Lieut A. McK. Johnstone No 3 section 51st (Highd) Divl Signal Co wounded.	
	4th, 5th		Everything quiet communication maintained	
	6th		Lieut R.G. Sellars No 4 section 51st (Highd) Divl Signal Co wounded.	
	7th to 15th		Very good communication was maintained with Brigade headqrs. (Roofs & ladders being formed to ensure this) On no occasion during this period was working interrupted	
	15th	540.	L/Cpl J Eustace wounded on 15th	
	16th, 17th		Brig. attack at Festubert Communication was maintained during the whole time of the attack	
	18th to 26th		Very quiet — communication maintained	
	27th		Division transferred to Indian Corps. Two cable sections left for La Nouveau Monde. Communication with Corps headquarters already established when we arrived	

WAR DIARY for month ending 30th June 1915. Army Form C. 2118.
or
INTELLIGENCE SUMMARY. 51st (High'd) Divl Signal Co.

(Erase heading not required.)

Place	Date	Hour	Summary of Events and Information	Remarks and references to Appendices
Laventie	JUNE 28th		Rest of company moved to La Nouveau Monde. Communication established with Brigade Headqrs. 152nd Inf Bde ⎫ 153rd Inf Bde ⎬ Laventie 154th Inf Bde ⎭ Picantin	
	29 + 30th		Everything quiet communications uninterrupted. During June the lines were patrolled every day.	

WAR DIARY for month ending 31st July 1915. Army Form C. 2118.

or

INTELLIGENCE SUMMARY.

(Erase heading not required.) 51st (Highld) Divl Signal Co

Place	Date	Hour	Summary of Events and Information	Remarks and references to Appendices
Field Ma YeA	July 1st to 14th		Nothing outstanding took place. Communication was maintained to Brigade headqrs without interruption	
	15th to 23rd		Cable was buried from Laventie to fortified post two miles distant. Communication was maintained throughout	
	24th		Attached to tenth Corps	
			System of communication was handed over to Lahore Divn and 8th Division	
	26th		Coy left La Gorgue station at 7 pm for Corbie arriving about 9.30 a.m on 27th and reached Heilly about 12 noon	
	27th		Telephone & Telegraph lines had already been laid to 10th Corps Hqrs. While detraining at Corbie two cyclist orderlies attached to unit from 51st (Highld) Divl Cyclist Co were injured — one subsequently dying in hospital	
	28th & 29th		Communication with Bde Hqrs carried on by motor cyclists 152nd Inf Bde Pont Noyelles 153rd Inf Bde Fréchencourt 154th Inf Bde Ribemont	

WAR DIARY for month ending 31st July 1915

or

INTELLIGENCE SUMMARY.
(Erase heading not required.)

51st (Highd) Divl Signal Co

Army Form C. 2118.

Instructions regarding War Diaries and Intelligence Summaries are contained in F. S. Regs., Part II. and the Staff Manual respectively. Title pages will be prepared in manuscript.

Place	Date	Hour	Summary of Events and Information	Remarks and references to Appendices
Field nr BPA	July 30th		Two cable sections left for Senlis to establish communication with Brigade Hqrs. 152nd Inf Bde Martinsart 153rd Inf Bde Mouledivilliers 154th Inf Bde Aveluy. As it was a very quiet part of the line that the 51st (Highd) Divn held during July communication was uninterrupted. Linemen patrolled Telegraph & Telephone lines every day.	

121/6743

51st Division

51st Signal Co. R.E.

Vol II

August 15

51st (Highld) Divl Signal Co. R.E.
Army Form C. 2118

WAR DIARY
or
INTELLIGENCE SUMMARY

For month ending 31st August 1915.

(Erase heading not required.)

Place	Date	Hour	Summary of Events and Information	Remarks and references to Appendices
Field.	1st to 3rd.		The two cable detachments which left Heilly for Senlis on 30th July were laying a new system of communication between Divisional Headqrs and Brigade Headqrs to replace the French system.	
	4th		Rest of company left Heilly for Senlis.	
	5th to 19th		Relieved the French Signal Company. Cable detachments and work parties improving communications to all Headqrs in Division.	
	20th		Thirteen men from Signal Depot forming a reinforcement for unit arrived on 8th. 20 line Telephone switchboard received.	
	21st to 31st.		Extra lines laid to Brigade Headquarters for telephonic communication. New lines were also laid to several units in Division, who previous to receipt of 20 line "Exchange" we were unable to put on switchboard. Communication during September August were ^very seldom interrupted and when so were quickly restored. The lines were patrolled every day by Linesmen.	

51st Division

51st Divl. Signal Co. RE.

Vol III

September 1915

Army Form C. 2118.

WAR DIARY 51st (Highd) Divl Signal Co RE

INTELLIGENCE SUMMARY September

(Erase heading not required.)

Instructions regarding War Diaries and Intelligence Summaries are contained in F.S. Regs., Part II. and the Staff Manual respectively. Title pages will be prepared in manuscript.

Place	Date	Hour	Summary of Events and Information	Remarks and references to Appendices
Field.	September 1st to 30th		During the month of September detachments were erecting air lines to replace the cable lines which had been previously laid down, the cable being subsequently reeled up. No 2, 3 & 4 sections while their Brigades were in action buried all their lines between Brigade Headquarters and the Battalions. Brigade Headqrs. Martinsart Aveluy. Hénencourt. Two men were at GHQ for instructional course in Wireless Telegraphy. This unit has now three men who are qualified in Wireless Telegraphy. Lieut. J. Spence accidentally hurt & admitted to hospital on 14th. 2nd Lieut. T.S. Hocking was transferred to 5th Divl Signal Co. on 16th. Communications were maintained satisfactorily during month, lines being patrolled every day.	

A. Whitton
MAJOR. R.E.T.
O.C. SIGNAL COY. H.Q. 51st.

121/7341

51st Division

51st Signal Coy R.E.
Vol IV
Oct 15

Army Form C. 2118.

October

WAR DIARY
or
INTELLIGENCE SUMMARY.
(Erase heading not required.)

Instructions regarding War Diaries and Intelligence Summaries are contained in F. S. Regs., Part II. and the Staff Manual respectively. Title pages will be prepared in manuscript.

Place	Date	Hour	Summary of Events and Information	Remarks and references to Appendices

Field.	October 1st. to 31st		As all the comic airlines were completed in September, during October every available man was employed building a stable which was completed by the end of the month. Communications (with the exception of a few minor faults) were uninterrupted. The lines were carefully patrolled every day, care being taken to strengthen any weak points. A reinforcement company the following officers arrived from 3/1st (Highland) Divisional Signal Coy Aberdeen.
			
			      " Lieut Akemp RE
			      " Lieut R.A. Robertson RE
			      " Lieut J.W. Laird RE,
			
			 Headqrs. 51st (Highd) Divl Signal Co. Senlis.
			      " Brigade Sections "
			      " No 4 Section 154th Infantry Brigade Avebury. (continuously)
				152nd & 153rd Bdes rotate between the two places Hebuterne (Rest billets) Mailly-Maillet (Trenches) Hebuterne Martinsart Avebury (continuously)

1577 Wt.W10791/1773 500,000 1/15 D.D.&L. A.D.S.S./Forms/C. 2118.

١٢١/٧٦٣٧

١٢ يوم
١
ذلك ؟ ن
١
لو مع
قيمته
ذلك

Army Form C. 2118.

WAR DIARY for November

~~INTELLIGENCE SUMMARY.~~

(Erase heading not required.)

Instructions regarding War Diaries and Intelligence Summaries are contained in F. S. Regs., Part II. and the Staff Manual respectively. Title pages will be prepared in manuscript.

Place	Date	Hour	Summary of Events and Information	Remarks and references to Appendices
Field	NOVR 1st to 30th		During the month Headquarters sections erected new lines to A.A. Silt Group at Bouzincourt and to the Alhambra Survey Post. All our lines were strengthened to withstand gale. The Brigade sections were engaged as follows :- (a) A new buried system was completed between Brigade Headquarters at Aveluy and Battalion Headquarters at Sector 72. (b) From Macmahon Post to Sectors G1 & G2 duplicate lines were buried (c) From Brigade Headquarters at Martinsart to Macmahon Post the wires which formerly were too close to each other were separated and now go by devious routes. (d) A wire was buried from the visual dugout beside Macmahon Post to the visual dugout at Railway & from there continued to the Brigade Headquarters at Aveluy and Martinsart Communications were practically uninterrupted during the month. All lines were patrolled very carefully every day by Divisional Linemen. Diagram of communications enclosed.	

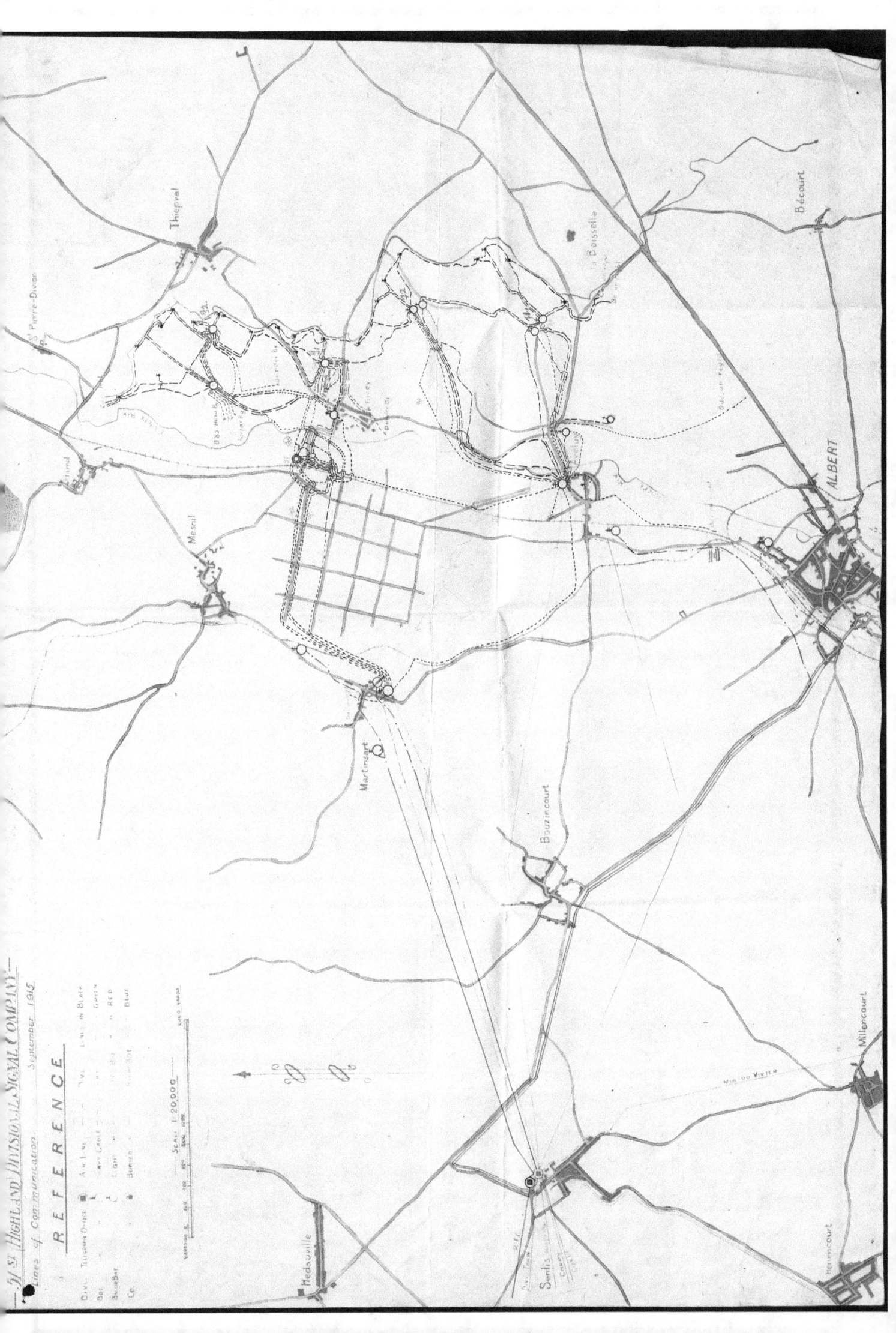

51st Div Signal Co. AEF

Dec
vol VI

Army Form C. 2118.

WAR DIARY
or
INTELLIGENCE SUMMARY.
(Erase heading not required.)

Place	Date	Hour	Summary of Events and Information	Remarks and references to Appendices
December	1st to		All wires running through Bouzencourt were straightened out and built on a fresh system amplifying that centre. A spur was built from the southern portion of the Corps trunk lines to Dernyfoits. These Corps lines in our area have been patrolled by our linemen. All lines from Bde Hqrs forward & particularly from Battn to Coy Hqrs have entailed a great deal of work & renewing of cable owing to the heavy rains and the work parties cutting lines while repairing trenches. On 23rd 152nd Inf Bde left Henencourt for Montigny and arrived at est billets in Vaux en Amienois on 25th. Communication was kept up by N.6 D.R.s. On 23rd 153nd Inf Bde left Aveluy for Henencourt leaving that place for Montigny on 29th and arrived at rest billets in Hallens du Bois on 30th. Communication being kept up by M.C. D.R.s. 96th Inf Bde relieved 152nd at Aveluy on 23rd & 96th Inf Bde occupied Henencourt on 29th, both Bdes belong to 32nd Divn. Communications were uninterrupted during the month. All lines were patrolled by linemen every day. Copy of communication enclosed. Aveluy	Divl Hqrs - Leahy { Bde Hqrs. Montluart Henencourt

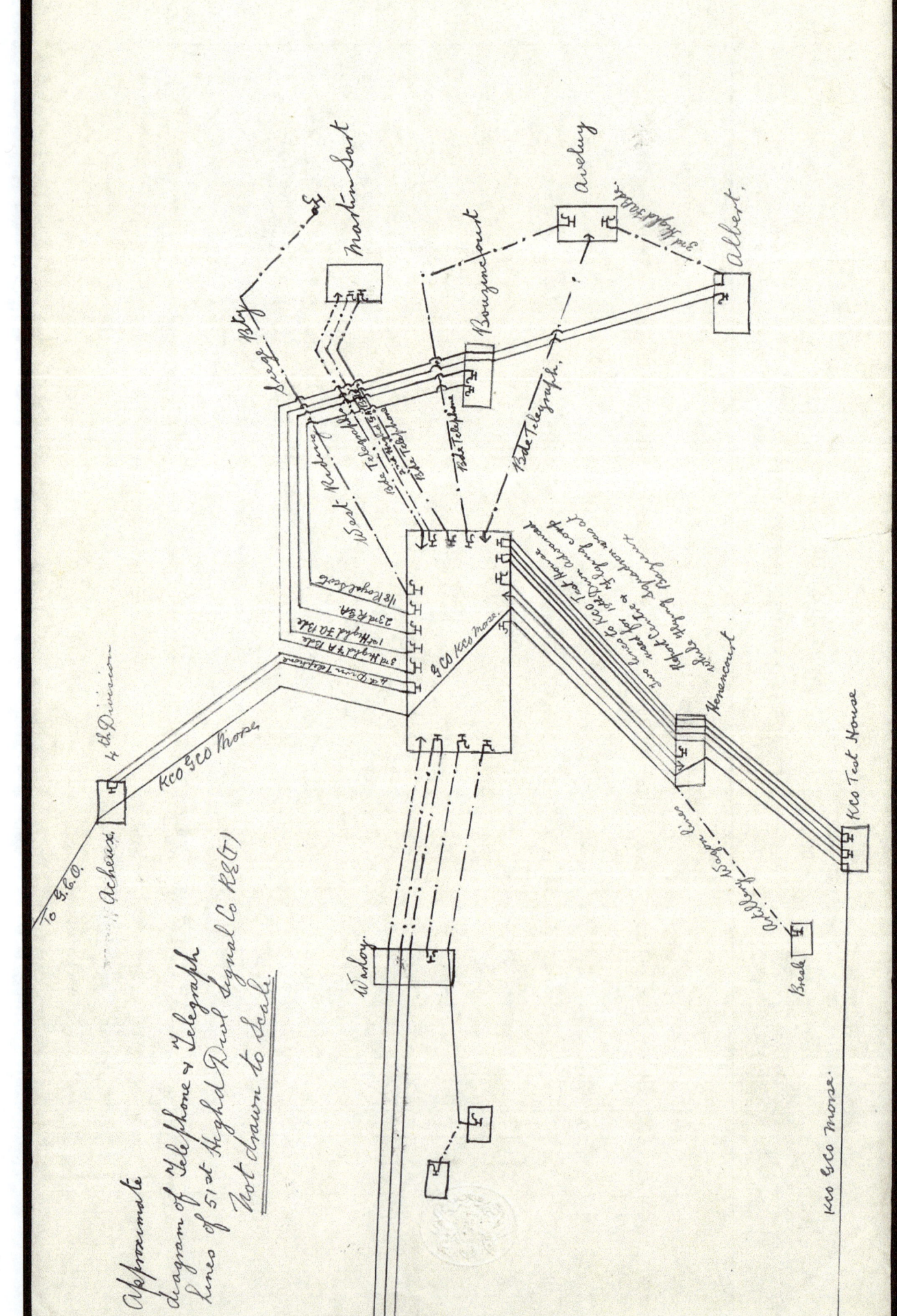

51

Signal Coy

Vol 7. 8. 9
& 10

Original.

Army Form C. 2118.

WAR DIARY of 51st (Highland) Divisional Signal Company R.E. (T).
or
INTELLIGENCE SUMMARY.
(Erase heading not required.)

Instructions regarding War Diaries and Intelligence Summaries are contained in F. S. Regs., Part II. and the Staff Manual respectively. Title pages will be prepared in manuscript.

Place	Date	Hour	Summary of Events and Information	Remarks and references to Appendices
	January 1916.			
Field	2nd.		The Division moved into rest area and the Signal Company was located at FLESSELLES. The location of the Brigade Signal Section was as follows:- 152nd Bde MOLLIENS AUX BOIS, 153rd Bde VAUX, 154 Bde MONTON VILLERS. Communication with the Brigades was by a comic airline system taken over from the 32nd Division supplemented by cables. During the month this comic airline was considerably strengthened and improved. Classes in signalling were organised for men of Infantry and artillery units and a considerable amount of instruction imparted. Refitting and overhauling instruments and transport was carried out.	
	18th		Three NCOs and 1 man were sent to Signal Training Centre for a candidates for commission in Signal units.	

Original

Army Form C. 2118.

WAR DIARY of 51st (Highland) Divisional Signal Company R.E. (T)

INTELLIGENCE SUMMARY

(Erase heading not required.)

Instructions regarding War Diaries and Intelligence Summaries are contained in F.S. Regs., Part II. and the Staff Manual respectively. Title pages will be prepared in manuscript.

Place	Date	Hour	Summary of Events and Information	Remarks and references to Appendices
Field	February. 1916.			
	3rd		13th Corps Headquarters moved and communication direct to 3rd Army substituted for that to 13th Corps.	
	8th		Division left rest area and Signal Company moved to DAOURS a detachment leaving the previous day for the purpose of building lines. Brigades at :- 152nd & 152nd CORBIE. 153rd ST GRATIEN. Communication with 152nd 152nd Bdes was by poled cable lines and with the 153rd Bde by Despatch Rider Service.	
	19th		153rd Bde to SAILLY-LE-SEC – communication still by Despatch Rider.	
	26th		153rd Bde moved up to BRAY and Telegraph & telephone communication was established through the 30th Divn system.	
	26th		Arrangements made to take over the 30th Divn system.	
	27th		Reinforcement of 13 O.R. from 3/1st Highland Divn Signal Coy.	
	29th		Relief of 30th Division cancelled and Division returned to Rest area. Signal Company again at FRESSELLIES	

1577 Wt. W10791/1773 500,000 1/15 D.D.&L. A.D.S.S./Forms/C. 2118.

Original

Page 1.

Army Form C. 2118.

WAR DIARY of 51st (Highland)
Divisional Signal Company
or
INTELLIGENCE SUMMARY. R.E.(T)

(Erase heading not required.)

Instructions regarding War Diaries and Intelligence
Summaries are contained in F. S. Regs., Part II.
and the Staff Manual respectively. Title pages
will be prepared in manuscript.

Place	Date	Hour	Summary of Events and Information	Remarks and references to Appendices
Field	March 1916			
	6th		The Company remained at LESSELLES until the 6th inst. The only communication established was a telephone circuit with a super-imposed morse direct to 3rd Army. The communications to the Brigades were maintained by Despatch Rider. The Divisional Headquarters moved to BEAUVAL & the Signal company was located in the same place. No telegraphic communication was established. 3rd Army Signal Office at BEAUVAL handed the traffic. Telephone communication was established through the 3rd Army Signals Exchange at BEAUVAL.	
	8th		No 1 Section of the Company went forward to build the communications and take over from the French in the ROCLINCOURT Sector. Temporary Divisional Headquarters were taken over from the French at DUISANS and cable lines laid out to advanced 153rd Bde "AUXREITZ" (left); 152nd Bde "MAROEUIL" (Reserve), and 154th Bde "ETRUN" (right)	
	9th		Headquarters moved to FREVENT.	

1577 Wt.W10791/1773 500,000 1/15 D. D. & L. A.D.S.S./Forms/C. 2118.

Original
Page 2.

Army Form C. 2118.

WAR DIARY
or
INTELLIGENCE SUMMARY.
(Erase heading not required.)

Instructions regarding War Diaries and Intelligence Summaries are contained in F. S. Regs., Part II. and the Staff Manual respectively. Title pages will be prepared in manuscript.

Place	Date	Hour	Summary of Events and Information	Remarks and references to Appendices
Field	March 1916 (Contd)			
	9th (contd)		Communication with 14th Corps was established by telephone and reinforced telegraph through PREVENT civil Post-Office. Communication with Brigades was by Despatch Rider. During the period 6th to 12th the Brigades were moving daily and consequently considerable strain devolved on the Signals. Communication however was uninterrupted.	
	12th		The Company Headquarters reported No 1 Section at PUISANS took up communication from here.	
	14th		Headquarters of the Division moved to HERMAVILLE according to that place. Company was established in that place. A Signal advanced report centre was fixed at ETRUN distribution to Brigades made from here. To Telephone Pairs and a more circuit were run to HERMAVILLE retaining the remainder of the month this system and as are in the forward area was strengthened.	[signature]
	29th		Buried cables were put in the forward area & a considerable amount of overhead line [illegible] by signals by [illegible] brigades	

1577 Wt. W10791/1773 500,000 1/15 D. D. & L. A.D.S.S./Forms/C. 2118.

Original

Army Form C. 2118.

WAR DIARY of 51st (Highland) Division Signal Company RE(T)

or

INTELLIGENCE SUMMARY.

(Erase heading not required.)

Place	Date	Hour	Summary of Events and Information	Remarks and references to Appendices
Field	April 1916		Communication arrangements so far the latter part of March. More buried lines were installed in the forward area and the forward area cleared of old French lines and overhead circuits generally. A permanent system carrying 7 conductors was run between HERMAVILLE and ETRUN and proved satisfactory. Lines in the forward area subjected to frequent, heavy shelling but no interruption of any note was caused.	
	22nd		Sapper W. J. Lyle wounded in left leg.	

Confidential

War Diaries
of the
51st (Highland) Divn Signal Coy
R.E.

From 1st May – 31st May 1916

Vol XI

Army Form C. 2118.

WAR DIARY
or
INTELLIGENCE SUMMARY.

(Erase heading not required.)

No 3093(A)
51st HIGHLAND DIVISION

Instructions regarding War Diaries and Intelligence Summaries are contained in F. S. Regs., Part II. and the Staff Manual respectively. Title pages will be prepared in manuscript.

Place	Date	Hour	Summary of Events and Information	Remarks and references to Appendices
Hem... 1st May to 31st May 1916			During May the communications were as for April and were with the exception of slight and temporary faults uninterrupted despite occasional heavy shelling.	

A Robertson
MAJOR, R.E.T.
O.C. SIGNAL COY. H.D.

Vol 12

Confidential

War Diaries
of the
51st (Highland) Division Signal Coy
R.E.
from 1st June to 30th June 1916

Army Form C. 2118.

WAR DIARY
or
INTELLIGENCE SUMMARY.
(Erase heading not required.)

Instructions regarding War Diaries and Intelligence Summaries are contained in F. S. Regs., Part II. and the Staff Manual respectively. Title pages will be prepared in manuscript.

CONFIDENTIAL
Nº 3092 (A)
HIGHLAND DIVISION.

Place	Date	Hour	Summary of Events and Information	Remarks and references to Appendices
Kemmel P.O.	June 1916		Early in June the 152nd Inf Bde took over the sector to the left of the 153rd Inf Bde. This caused some considerable rearrangement of lines in the forward area. The change was accomplished without any difficulty though it was necessary to construct another short stretch of permanent line to effect the necessary junctions. 2/Lt W. GALLOWAY joined as a reinforcement from 3/1st Highland Divisional Signal Coy on the 3 inst	

A Austen
O.C. SIGNAL COY. H.D.

MAJOR R.E.
O.C. SIGNAL COY. H.D.

1577 Wt. W10791/1773 500,000 1/15 D. D. & L. A.D.S.S./Forms/C. 2118.

Vol 13

Confidential

War Diaries
of the
51st (Highland) Division Signal Coy
R.E.T.
from 1st July 16 to 31st July 1916

WAR DIARY or INTELLIGENCE SUMMARY.

Army Form C. 2118.

No. 3092(A)

Place	Date	Hour	Summary of Events and Information	Remarks and references to Appendices
Reynauld P.C.	1st to 14th		Sections of the technical personnel of the 60th Divn Signal Coy were attached for instruction	
"	14th	10am	Communications and Signal Office handed over to 60th Divn Signal Coy.	
Villers Chatel	14th	10am	Office opened. Wire lines to (1) 17th Pd Pd + 152 Inf Bde (2) 153rd Inf Bde 154 Inf Bde.	
			Telephone line to 17th Cdn F.A.S.	
DOULLENS	15th	9am	Office opens. Morse line to Third Army. Telephone comm. thro' Doullens Civil Exchange.	
RIBEAUCOURT Dept SOMME	16th	9am	Office opens. Communication established with Reserve Army at 4hr. By morse and telephone. No lines to Brigades all wires by DR	
"	17th		Ditto	
"	18th		Ditto	
"	19th	8pm	Transport and Company less details marches to FLESSELLES.	
RIBEMONT	20th	12noon	Drum All Company arrived and Signal Office opened. Morse line and telephone communication with 15th Pd Pd Pd.	
	21st →			

Army Form C. 2118.

WAR DIARY
or
INTELLIGENCE SUMMARY.
(Erase heading not required.)

Instructions regarding War Diaries and Intelligence Summaries are contained in F. S. Regs., Part II. and the Staff Manual respectively. Title pages will be prepared in manuscript.

Place	Date	Hour	Summary of Events and Information	Remarks and references to Appendices
FRICOURT	22nd	11pm	Office in CHATEAU DUGOUT taken over from 33rd Divnl Signal Company. Lines as follows: telephone and move to 18th to 9 a Buzzer to 154th & 153rd Bdes in valley East of MAMETZ.	
	24th		All lines very difficult to maintain owing to heavy barrage, fire constantly on valley. Runners reverted to with good results.	
	25th		Visual posts established and communication by two means with both Bdes & Divnl HQrs maintained.	
	27th		Wireless installed at both Bdes and working to a wireless station at FRICOURT. Casualties from 22nd to 31st. 2 O.R. Killed 1 O.R. Missing 16 O.R. Wounded (5 gassed)	

A. [signature]

MAJOR. R.E.T.
O.C. SIGNAL COY. H.D.

51st Divisional Engineers

51st (Highland) DIVISIONAL SIGNAL COMPANY R.E

AUGUST 1916

WAR DIARY
or
INTELLIGENCE SUMMARY.
(Erase heading not required.)

Army Form C. 2118.

CONFIDENTIAL
No 30977 31/A
HIGHLAND DIVISION

Place	Date	Hour	Summary of Events and Information	Remarks and references to Appendices
Field	1st – 6th August 1916		Operations by Division in Somme Valley were continued with Infantry Brigade Headquarters and Artillery Brigade Headquarters by Telegraph and Telephone was maintained satisfactorily. As the lines were broken so frequently by shell fire, it was found expedient to make use of a laddering system in the shell swept areas. This was found to give good results & the lines worked through with little or no interruption. It also saved considerable work for the linemen, who had merely to repair the ladder each day & this could be done at the most propitious time. Despatch Riders were also employed between Divisional Headquarters and Infantry Brigade Headquarters but owing to the very rough condition of the roads, their running was reduced to a minimum. The communications from Brigade forward were by telephone and telegraph in part but visual signalling had to be resorted to on frequent occasions when the sole means of communication bet. telegraph and telephone lines the laddering system was adopted.	[signature]

1577 Wt. W10791/1773 500,000 1/15 D.D.&L. A.D.S.S./Forms/C.2118.

Army Form C. 2118.

WAR DIARY
— or —
INTELLIGENCE SUMMARY.
(Erase heading not required.)

Instructions regarding War Diaries and Intelligence Summaries are contained in F. S. Regs., Part II. and the Staff Manual respectively. Title pages will be prepared in manuscript.

Place	Date	Hour	Summary of Events and Information	Remarks and references to Appendices
Field	1st – 6th August 1916 (contd)		Flags, discs & lamps were used in Vaux. Cyclists and foot orderlies were of necessity employed to a considerable extent. There was also established visual communication between Divisional Headquarters and Brigade Headquarters, but it was not required. Communication with 15th Corps was uninterrupted.	S.
Field	6th – 9th August 1916		On 6th inst. Division moved out of action and no fresh signal office at RIBEMONT. Communication to Infantry Brigades was mainly by D.R.L.S., but a Signal Office was installed at DERNANCOURT connected by wire to Divisional Signal Office and part of the work for Brigades distributed from there.	S.
Field	9th – 12th August 1916		Communication with 15th Corps was as usual.	S.

(signed) Spencer Ho/T/C

1577 Wt. W10791/1773 500,000 1/15 D. D. & L.   A.D.S.S./Forms/C. 2118.

Army Form C. 2118.

WAR DIARY
or
INTELLIGENCE SUMMARY.
(Erase heading not required.)

Instructions regarding War Diaries and Intelligence Summaries are contained in F. S. Regs., Part II. and the Staff Manual respectively. Title pages will be prepared in manuscript.

Place	Date	Hour	Summary of Events and Information	Remarks and references to Appendices
Field	9th - 12th August 1916		On 9th inst. Divisional Headquarters moved to PONT REMY into 10th Corps area. No telegraph or telephone communication was ever kept with Corps. Divisional communications were by despatch rider & cyclist orderly.	X.
Field	12th - 18th August 1916		Divisional Headquarters moved to RENESCURE on 12th inst. into 2nd Anzac Corps area. Communication by telephone was established with Infantry Brigades. Corps communication was by telephone and the usual D.R.L.S. On 15th inst. 1 officer & a detachment of linemen were sent to ARMENTIERES to look over New Zealand Division communications with view to takingover.	S.
Field	18th - 29th August 1916		Signal Office was opened at ARMENTIERES on 18th inst. We took over the existing system of communications from the New Zealand Divisional Signal	[signature]

A.D.S.S./Forms/C. 2118.

Army Form C. 2118.

WAR DIARY
or
INTELLIGENCE SUMMARY.
(Erase heading not required.)

Place	Date	Hour	Summary of Events and Information	Remarks and references to Appendices
Lila	18th – 29th August (contd)		Signal Company. This was a Panel system of communications throughout the town. No wires were for the most part in rivers. There was on each leakage on some lines in the sewers. This was due mainly to inferior cable and was eliminated to a great extent. The usual Despatch Rider Service was employed, much work fell on cyclist orderlies with delivered throughout the town. Both communications as usual.	
Lila	29th – 31st August 1916		Divisional Headquarters moved to STEENWERCK on 29th inst and our office opened here, a 30 line Exchange being left at ARMENTIERES. for working to Infantry Brigades and dealing with work for units in that town. There was also a 30 line Exchange left here for Artillery work. Several lines had to be laid as some units of 51st Division were left in front positions.	

Army Form C. 2118.

WAR DIARY
or
INTELLIGENCE SUMMARY.
(Erase heading not required.)

Place	Date	Hour	Summary of Events and Information	Remarks and references to Appendices
Casualties			No 446 M/C Cpl M. Stewart slight wound on head 2/8/16.	A.A.
Honours			No 754 Sergeant Alexander Gavin awarded military medal 15/8/16.	
			No 492 Sergeant Duncan Mackenzie awarded military medal 16/8/16.	

CONFIDENTIAL.
No. 21/A.
HIGHLAND
DIVISION.

War Diary.
— for —
51st (High.) Divisional Signal
Co. R.E. (T)
— for —
September
1916.

CONFIDENTIAL

Army Form C. 2118.

WAR DIARY
or
INTELLIGENCE SUMMARY.
(Erase heading not required.)

Place	Date	Hour	Summary of Events and Information	Remarks and references to Appendices
Field	1st to 22nd		During this period the Divisional Headquarters were at STEENWERCK, and the Signal Company work consisted in maintaining the existing system of communications.	A
			There were four telephone exchanges in use viz:- at STEENWERCK and three in ARMENTIERES (including one for artillery)	B
			A report centre was set up in ARMENTIERES and was responsible for working of communications forward to Brigade Headquarters.	
			A panel system of communication was in vogue from this report centre forward and was found to be rather involved. Most of the lines ran in sewers throughout the town and as V.5. cable had been extensively used, great difficulty was experienced in combating the earth leakage. Sound cables were utilised in some places.	C
			Two Brigade Headquarters were in ARMENTIERES and one in STEEN-WERCK. All three were on our telephone exchanges.	D
			Telephone communication with the Right Brigade. There were a number of Corps and Army troops in this area.	E

Army Form C. 2118.

2.

WAR DIARY
or
INTELLIGENCE SUMMARY.
(Erase heading not required.)

Place	Date	Hour	Summary of Events and Information	Remarks and references to Appendices

and as it was essential that these should be linked up with their respective centres, they had to be put on our switchboards. 9.

The permanent route between STEENWERCK and that put ARMENTIERS was strengthened and otherwise improved. 9.

Burying of wires forward of advanced Brigade Headquarters was proceeded with. Difficulty was experienced in digging trenches 6' deep owing to the presence of water. 9.

V.R.L. service was maintained as usual. There were extensive deliveries by Cyclist Orderlies both at ARMENTIERES and STEENWERCK. 9.

The erection of stables and horse standings for the wurkul was commenced. Captain B.E. Cote R.E. came from 2nd Army Signals and took over temporary Command of company as from 1/th September 1916. 9.

James Sterman Capos

Army Form C. 2118.

WAR DIARY
or
INTELLIGENCE SUMMARY.
(Erase heading not required.)

Instructions regarding War Diaries and Intelligence Summaries are contained in F. S. Regs., Part II. and the Staff Manual respectively. Title pages will be prepared in manuscript.

Place	Date	Hour	Summary of Events and Information	Remarks and references to Appendices
Stonude	22nd	6.0 pm	Capt Stevenson joined the Coy from 18th Coy. Signed by to take over command of Coy. Information received that 37th Div would hand over the line to France Div on 25th inst and was arranged that Coy Coy should continue to take charge of our ammunition until that date. 51st Div transportation move to Tatou. Signal Office is established on culvert N. of chateau one on terrace in town alongside. Clear the mesed regarders to forward.	
	23rd	"		
	26th	"		
	29th	"	Operation orders recd that Division would proceed to Doncourt. Detachment of Coy section D.H. Company under Lt Brown leave by train to join the Divisional Arty at Picturelho	
	30th	"	The Offices is closed at Tata at 10.0 am and opened at Beauval at 12. noon. The company entrain at Ballent for Doullens out instructions	

1577 Wt. W10791/1773 500,000 1/15 D. D. & L.   A.D.S.S./Forms/C. 2118.

Army Form C. 2118.

WAR DIARY
or
INTELLIGENCE SUMMARY.

(Erase heading not required.)

Instructions regarding War Diaries and Intelligence Summaries are contained in F. S. Regs., Part II. and the Staff Manual respectively. Title pages will be prepared in manuscript.

Place	Date	Hour	Summary of Events and Information	Remarks and references to Appendices
			To proceed to Brussel on arrival from Steamer Copice at 51st Div hounds.	

1577 Wt.W10791/1773 500,000 1/15 D. D. & L. A.D.S.S./Forms/C. 2118.

Army Form C. 2118.

CONFIDENTIAL
No. 21/2.
HIGHLAND DIVI⁵

1/51ˢᵗ (Highland) Division Sig Cory
October 1916
Signal Coy

WAR DIARY
or
INTELLIGENCE SUMMARY.
(Erase heading not required.)

Place	Date	Hour	Summary of Events and Information	Remarks and references to Appendices
Beauval	1ˢᵗ		Instructions received that Company would proceed to Beauval by Motor. That Hd of Company that had travelled from Ostre on night of 28/9/16 improved and motorists knew to Beauval. Officer checked Beauval and found at Beauval. The officer then was detained in a broken lorry, in the park behind the Chateau. His car broke down late in the Royal behind the Hotel and was detained on the Exponent State. The Officer was finally lent over by an Exponent officer and two more Lieutenants & Corps. as broken accepted by Brigade in line. There was arms and made of Humous Eric and Humours fell at some time Chemin on and present on Luverne. From there he heard him tell at no time been seen & the news the Luvecogole. The Cyclie Section for Lillers went to	

Army Form C. 2118.

WAR DIARY
or
INTELLIGENCE SUMMARY.
(Erase heading not required.)

Instructions regarding War Diaries and Intelligence Summaries are contained in F. S. Regs., Part II. and the Staff Manual respectively. Title pages will be prepared in manuscript.

Place	Date	Hour	Summary of Events and Information	Remarks and references to Appendices
			within a short distance of the trenches and covered by his own letter trenches and several connecting trench. Not even. There have been at present ½ the left deeply entrenched than to N of St Simon. There are also three advanced trenches. The front lines are up to C.P. system and the 2nd and 3rd lines are a few ovarians. There had (the trenches) been all. There was many not taken by the rifle action but at present DBr G, by the C.P. bommand the system not the trenches a central trench can any from B beyond on to C.P. system to the By onto the trust as a forward Bayon headquarters in Pope Trench. From these lines were carried trusted on the new environment trench to the forward Bayon headquarters a talue a for them by the work to the hostile. A considerable amount of difficulty was experienced in doing this owing to the ordinary	

1577 Wt.W10791/1773 500,000 1/15 D.D.&L. A.D.S.S./Forms/C. 2118.

Army Form C. 2118.

WAR DIARY
or
INTELLIGENCE SUMMARY.
(Erase heading not required.)

Instructions regarding War Diaries and Intelligence Summaries are contained in F. S. Regs., Part II. and the Staff Manual respectively. Title pages will be prepared in manuscript.

Place	Date	Hour	Summary of Events and Information	Remarks and references to Appendices
Bus	2	3pm	9th the trenches our horse was shelled on 7th and one man killed on 8th. In addition there were 17 cases some severe cases by shrapnel. The lines and road are liable to the date, regiment but are not let out the dugouts as they were not completed before it became off the line. 3rd Cav. transport from trenches to Reserve.	
"	3	3.30pm	Arrived here left on Kaplan carriage of horses. Horse suffering considerably. There were considerable congestion down Kitchen lull taking the horse to put through. Trough on horse to 3rd Cav.	
"	4	"	Trough on Kaplan and horse to 13th Cav. de Ypres.	
"	18.	"	Officer came at Bus operated Relieve. Shrapnel at Relieve was taken on from 6.30 pm. Helmes K Brigade were supplied by Cav. on other land	

1577 Wt.W10791/1773 500,000 1/15 D. D. & L. A.D.S.S./Forms/C. 2118.

WAR DIARY
or
INTELLIGENCE SUMMARY.
(Erase heading not required.)

Army Form C. 2118.

Place	Date	Hour	Summary of Events and Information	Remarks and references to Appendices
	21		All the permanent roads remain. Approved offices were established at Ali Jordan having turned for their own use much of G. Agyeh or the system. From the formed system of roads have had have been at a Base and Bc Base Compounds. There have been houses to kept in for of commanding that there were other but have been constantly taken to trucks & the area some entrances & exits & still for and the traffic for outages. A General Rhot Curt was constituted at Howrah all has been most unable to not coming not the for shelter of the Company as there the billets are kept.	

CONFIDENTIAL

VOL 17

War Diary
51st (H) Divl. Signal Co.

1st November to 30 November 1916.

VOL 25.

Army Form C. 2118.

WAR DIARY
or
INTELLIGENCE SUMMARY.
(Erase heading not required.)

Place	Date	Hour	Summary of Events and Information	Remarks and references to Appendices
Fauburg Nd. 12th – 13th			Work continued in laying and maintaining lines and systems. A few lines were continually destroyed by shell fire. Brigade lines were laid right up to the line in anticipation of an advance. Almost all the work had to be done during the night.	
	12 M.		Office opened at Toncville & Mailly Maillet. Office kept open at Fauburg N. to deal with Administration work. Linemen sent to various posts & kept posts in readiness for the attack.	
	13		Infantry attacked at daylight. Communication remained good. We had to apply to the Corps for mounted orderlies as the roads (owing to the traffic & weather conditions) were impossible for motor cycles. Corps were already using	

Army Form C. 2118.

WAR DIARY
or
INTELLIGENCE SUMMARY.
(Erase heading not required.)

Place	Date	Hour	Summary of Events and Information	Remarks and references to Appendices
	14.		mounted orderlies	
	15.		12 men of I Corps Cavalry sent. Attacks continued, considerable resistance offered. Officer observed at Domuill. A portion of the company returned to Jenkillers.	
	17.		Some pigeon messages were sent during the advance but most of the work was done by mounted orderlies & was most satisfactory. 154 Bde. was relieved by a Bde. of the 32nd Divn. German motorcyclists captured during the advance were sent received. Lieut E.N. Cummins who was in charge of 153 Bde. section this day transferred to II Corps Heavy Arty.	
	18.		153rd Bde. moved to Ranichingal.	
	22.		Information received that Divn. would move to Mons Pill. on 23rd inst. and Divn. Arty. to Puba.	

Army Form C. 2118.

WAR DIARY
or
INTELLIGENCE SUMMARY.
(Erase heading not required.)

Instructions regarding War Diaries and Intelligence Summaries are contained in F. S. Regs., Part II. and the Staff Manual respectively. Title pages will be prepared in manuscript.

Place	Date	Hour	Summary of Events and Information	Remarks and references to Appendices
			and the positions frequently occupied by the 4th Canadians.	
	24		153 Bde moved to Puchvillers. Line extended from Raincheval to new Bde Hqrs. Pty detachment under Lieut J Bruce left for Aloux. Hdls at 8.30 A.M. Office closed at Mailly Maillet. 152 Bde moved to Toutencourt. 153 Bde moved to Headville.	
	26		5 Military Medals awarded to runners	
	27		Detachment under Lieut R. Gould proceeded to Nona Hill to take over from 4th Canadians. Party sent to Aveluy to establish Court open in exchange	
	28		Company moved to Nona Hill. Billets & Horse lines	

1577 Wt.W10791/1773 500,000 1/15 D. D. & L. A.D.S.S./Forms/C. 2118.

Army Form C. 2118.

WAR DIARY
or
INTELLIGENCE SUMMARY.
(Erase heading not required.)

Instructions regarding War Diaries and Intelligence Summaries are contained in F. S. Regs., Part II. and the Staff Manual respectively. Title pages will be prepared in manuscript.

Place	Date	Hour	Summary of Events and Information	Remarks and references to Appendices
at Wolseley Huts	29		Party sent to trace out all lines in forward areas. Signal Office is in and out. Men detailed to intercom offices and lines.	
	30		Two linesmen sent to "H" Dugout. Company Officer went on fire this morning. Many important documents lost, including important notes for War Diary. Party sent to Coln in arlern to assist with search lines.	

James Stevenson
Capt 185
O.C. 51st (H) Div Sig Co
RE.

CONFIDENTIAL.
No 21(A)
HIGHLAND
DIVISION.

Vol 18

War Diary
of
51st (Highland) Divisional Signal Co.
from 1st December, 1916.
to 31st December, 1916.

51st Division Signal Company — WAR DIARY or INTELLIGENCE SUMMARY
Army Form C. 2118. CONFIDENTIAL. No 71(A) HIGHLAND DIVISION.
December 1916

Place	Date	Hour	Summary of Events and Information	Remarks and references to Appendices
Vieux	1st		Renewed and out to the lines in Divisional area. Remainder of Company employed in repairing huts used as Offices and huts to Company offices and on fire by airway to detective structure of fireplace.	
	2nd		Company continued same work as yesterday.	
	3rd		152nd Inf. Bde. relieved 153 Bde. in line. Company employed cable work to new and clear away dead lines.	
	4		Antiphone exchange opened at Infantry H.Q. New Company augmented lines as estimated. Brigade transport lines. The Divisional teamsters and R.E. Company at whatever was there are connected to this exchange.	
	5		Company continues always to keep dressed cable and communication to repaired until road at Cable Shee. lines in N.W. side of Allies, Bapaume Road.	

Army Form C. 2118.

WAR DIARY
or
INTELLIGENCE SUMMARY.
(Erase heading not required.)

Place	Date	Hour	Summary of Events and Information	Remarks and references to Appendices
Flers	6.		Company continues work serving burial cables and maintaining track route	
	7-14		- do -	
	15.		Burial system trench from Flers to Eny, and as by O.C. cannot bear party on horse line party sent out to hy. cannot bear party on horse line party sent out from cables between trench.	
	17.		Lt Bruce proceeds to attend wireless course at G.H.Q. house school. Lt Galloway returns from acting as instructor at 5th Army Signal School. Additional cables run between Baal & Guyents a buried system.	
	19.			
	20.		Party sent out to maintain Tower cables between P+Q depots. enemy party lay armoured cable on ground between headquarters. Brigade to Luci and B depot on headquarters & Poziers. this continues from A depot on army system to Brig rest at Contalmaison and these circuit sic last established.	

1577 Wt. W10791/1773 500,000 1/15 D. D. & L. A.D.S.S./Forms/C. 2118.

WAR DIARY
or
INTELLIGENCE SUMMARY.
(Erase heading not required.)

Army Form C. 2118.

Place	Date	Hour	Summary of Events and Information	Remarks and references to Appendices
Kut	21		Headquarters. Above line toted. Party sent out to take out overhead lines.	
	22		Remainder of Company lay overhead line between depot & O.P.s. Inst. system shed the trenches are cut.	
	23		Cleaning up and calls to extend and renewing of buried lines.	
	24		to	
	25		C. Bros returned from SWB trenches lines.	
	26		Maintenance party on local line, also Brigaid reconnoitering.	
			Advanced line laid between said depot & buried system. Then line laid to Bn. OP. arty.	
	27		party stay permanent with F. line battl. It is difficult but they all must stand hard trench. Paths owing to wet both ways.	
	28		Line broken between OP dugout. Were am attempt broke in and was relaid.	
	29		Maintenance party & new line laid a reinforcement of yesterday.	

Army Form C. 2118.

WAR DIARY
or
INTELLIGENCE SUMMARY.
(Erase heading not required.)

Instructions regarding War Diaries and Intelligence Summaries are contained in F. S. Regs., Part II. and the Staff Manual respectively. Title pages will be prepared in manuscript.

Place	Date	Hour	Summary of Events and Information	Remarks and references to Appendices
[illegible]	29	a.m.	[illegible]	
	30		Operational conf. sent of police orders to war Diamond	
	31		Headquarters.	
			Diagram of our attacks	
			[signature] Lieut. Col. R.E.	

1577 Wt. W10791/1773 500,000 1/15 D. D. & L.   A.D.S.S./Forms/C. 2118.

Army Form C. 2118

CONFIDENTIAL
No 27 (A)
HIGHLAND DIVISION.

WAR DIARY
or
INTELLIGENCE SUMMARY
(Erase heading not required.)

Vol 19

War Diary.
51st (Highland) Divisional Signal Co.

from 1st January, 1917.
to 31st January, 1917.

51st Divisional Signal Co.

WAR DIARY
or
INTELLIGENCE SUMMARY.
(Erase heading not required.)

Army Form C. 2118.

January 1917

CONFIDENTIAL
No. 71(A)
HIGHLAND DIVISION.

Instructions regarding War Diaries and Intelligence Summaries are contained in F. S. Regs., Part II. and the Staff Manual respectively. Title pages will be prepared in manuscript.

Place	Date	Hour	Summary of Events and Information	Remarks and references to Appendices
Mons Mill	1st		Lines all correct. No working parties out.	
	2nd		Construction section ran up new lines along Albert-Bapaume Rd.	
	3rd		Work of clearing away disused cables continues. I.T. Out and forward offices by 3rd Army Buried Cable Company installed at Laurencie. This set was installed for purpose of (testing) the signals from to forms bigger at ten points to front line.	
			Instructions for handling the use of telephone in forward area issued to each unit in forward Div Sector.	
			O.C. 2nd Divisional Signal Company visited Mons and went over the system & lines with a view to taking them over when division is relieved.	4 5
			Work on clearing up disused cable continued -do-	

3rd Signal, 3rd Army install Signal Office and headquarts of brigades

Army Form C. 2118.

WAR DIARY
or
INTELLIGENCE SUMMARY.
(Erase heading not required.)

Instructions regarding War Diaries and Intelligence Summaries are contained in F. S. Regs., Part II. and the Staff Manual respectively. Title pages will be prepared in manuscript.

Place	Date	Hour	Summary of Events and Information	Remarks and references to Appendices
Mons	5th		Line work between IT off and forward buzzer successfully installed	
	6th		Took on clearing of cable overhead	
			Artillery detachment of 22nd Divisional Signal Company reported to the own arty lines	
	7th		Kept on clearing up cables overhead	
			of 11th British Signal Company. Took over arty communications	
			Lt Walker and 13 men from 2nd Div Signal Co R.E. arrived and are	
			attached to this company to learn how to use the airline	
			Mobile pigeon loft arrived for use 2 this division	
	8th		Infantry brade pigeon left drawn up to H.Q. near Signal Office	
			Mobile pigeon loft drawn up to H.Q. hill near Signal Office	
			Pioneers sent out on lines and buzzer from Divl.	
			Signal Company	
	9th		Maintenance party sent out on Indloits	
			buzzer overhead	

Army Form C. 2118.

WAR DIARY
or
INTELLIGENCE SUMMARY.
(Erase heading not required.)

Instructions regarding War Diaries and Intelligence Summaries are contained in F. S. Regs., Part II. and the Staff Manual respectively. Title pages will be prepared in manuscript.

Place	Date	Hour	Summary of Events and Information	Remarks and references to Appendices
Henencourt	10		Maintenance party continue work on instrument Position cells issued to all telephone stations	
	11 } 12 }		Company employed packing up stores preparatory to move to Berguy.	
	13		Company move to Berguy. Signal officer & men handed in & quarters at 11.0 am	
	14		Officer stencil horses same kind. Company now has horses & harness & Brevill. Officer start horses 11.0 am from Brevill came home.	
	15		Company hiked from Brevill to Berguy. Officer closed at Brevill, 12 noon Rene Berguy came in.	
	16		Company clean up billets. Signal Officer established in attic over entrance Château Company billets in form attentive below for one electric farm about ¾ mile west Vadelain-	

1577 Wt.W10791/1773 500,000 1/15 D. D. & L. A.D.S.S./Forms/C. 2118.

Army Form C. 2118.

WAR DIARY
or
INTELLIGENCE SUMMARY.
(Erase heading not required.)

Instructions regarding War Diaries and Intelligence Summaries are contained in F.S. Regs., Part II. and the Staff Manual respectively. Title pages will be prepared in manuscript.

Place	Date	Hour	Summary of Events and Information	Remarks and references to Appendices
Burgny	17		Recruits for Company are not satisfactory ostensibly owing to Lates and Marsall not men of authority in districts to traverse for them. Lts. Lam Bernard to knuyst is unstated and their time to be shown and noted by the Company.	
	18		Class for Visual Signalling & Sketches and Company format.	
	19		Company employed on billets. Visual Signal Wherever class	
	22		for men of H Company continued. Two Cinemas and 5 attended & Corps Signal School.	
	23		Instruction classes continued	
	24		Attended lecture on Trench System of Communications at Wiesden & Licester and Review left a new & proxy on Crest to an 9/3rd Trench Army	
	25		Took over some lines in area 9/3rd Trend Army. Both very regular hours expect on construction Cinque phases to Heyoth and beyond to GP Headquarters.	
	26/27		Classes for Divisional Signal Cy continued	

Army Form C. 2118.

WAR DIARY
or
INTELLIGENCE SUMMARY.
(Erase heading not required.)

Instructions regarding War Diaries and Intelligence Summaries are contained in F. S. Regs., Part II. and the Staff Manual respectively. Title pages will be prepared in manuscript.

Place	Date	Hour	Summary of Events and Information	Remarks and references to Appendices
Bagni	28th		Arrived Signal School established at Inead Bonio's men drawn from Infantry Bdy and twelve officers. She divided into 9 classes. Instructors from 6 Bdys. Royal Artillery, Highland, and Eni. work. Course for 15 days. Two officers visited men doing Signal Duty at as instructors taken 9 class attached Class. Instructors entrained.	
	29.31.		James Stevens Capt. R. A. O/c Signal School C.	

51st Divisional Signal School.

Programme of Work.

	Officers Class.	1	2	3	4	5	6	7	8
				NCO's & Men.					
9 - 10 am.	F.D.	L.W.	L.W.	L.W.	B.	B.	B.	F.D.	F.D.
10 - 11 am.	B.	F.D.	F.D.	F.D.	L.W.	L.W.	L.W.	B.	B.
11 - 12 Noon	L.W.	B.	B.	B.	F.D.	F.D.	F.D.	L.W.	L.W.
Noon - 1 pm.	L.	L.	L.	L.	L.	PR+S.	PR+S.	F.D.	F.D.
2 - 3 pm.	PR+S.	PR+S.	PR+S.	PR+S.	D.L.	B.	B.	B.	B.
3 - 4 pm.	D.L.	D.L.	D.L.	D.L.	B.	L.	L.	L.	L.

F.D. - Flag Drill. Station Work.
L.W. - Line Work.
B. - Buzzer.
L. - Lecture.
D.L. - Day Lamp.
PR+S. - Reading & Sending: Pairs.

CONFIDENTIAL.
****

WAR DIARY.

of

51st (Highland) Divisional Signal Co., R.E.

from 1st February, 1917 to 28th February, 1917.

Army Form C. 2118

CONFIDENTIAL
No 71(A)
HIGHLAND DIVISION.

WAR DIARY
or
INTELLIGENCE SUMMARY
(Erase heading not required.)

10 pm 18/3/17

Place	Date	Hour	Summary of Events and Information	Remarks and references to Appendices
Bugny Marlou	1st-3rd		Signalling Classes continued. W.	
	3rd		Classes finished. Personnel reported their units. W.	
	4th		Company employed packing wagons preparing to leaving Bugny St Marlou W	
	5		Left Bugny St Marlou and proceeded to Bailly. Office closed at Bugny St Marlou at 9.30 and opened at Bailly same road. W	
	6.		Left Bailly and proceeded to Inchem-le-Grand. Office closed at Bailly at 12 noon and opened at Inchem-le-Grand same road. Office in Mairie. W	
	7.		Left Inchem-le-Grand and proceeded to Rollencourt. Office closed at 12 noon at Inchem-le-Grand and opened at Rollencourt same road. W	
	8.		Left Rollencourt and proceeded to Nollier Chât. Office in hut near Château. W.	
	9.		Detachment laid line to E. RA at La Comte	

WAR DIARY
or
INTELLIGENCE SUMMARY
(Erase heading not required.)

Army Form C. 2118

Place	Date	Hour	Summary of Events and Information	Remarks and references to Appendices
	9		Guns laid to Bde in action MAROEUIL and to W. Bde in support RCA. W	
	10		Lines through to S.S.O. Mingoval. W	
	11		15th Bde arrived at Ag lines CRK. Went patrolled on Road lines W	
	12		Am put on Road Telegraph Poles (local). 5th Galloway out too men to get Cathorn to occur. R.G.O. on buried cables. W	
	13		Major Gen Gould Signal Offr. W. Captain laid down to join parade on an buried route. Saptum. There being no forward land communication to each divn. The alternative route in Anyon Tunnel. The party to bury alternative route in Anyon Tunnel. The	
	14		E.18D objected to this on the ground that the trench would be destroyed. There being no working party available. W	

Army Form C. 2118

WAR DIARY
or
INTELLIGENCE SUMMARY   3

(Erase heading not required.)

Instructions regarding War Diaries and Intelligence Summaries are contained in F.S. Regs., Part II. and the Staff Manual respectively. Title Pages will be prepared in manuscript.

Place	Date	Hour	Summary of Events and Information	Remarks and references to Appendices
			available to dig a splinter trench. Instructions were received to bury cable 9 inches in the foot of the trench. W.	
	15.		Applied for information as to Bde. Hqrs. These not yet fixed. Asked for party to bury to Role Hqrs. This was provided. Three detachments left Villers Chatel for Eegouves W.	
	16.		Party commenced work on overhead route forward of advanced S.end Hqrs in 2 squads at Cambry at Maroeuil and in leading in lines from Cab. route. Examined trenches forward of Right Bde. Hqrs. for cable route to Rlwy. W.	
	17.		Work continued on overhead route. Y	
	18.		— do — Horses returned from Eegouves there being no	

WAR DIARY or INTELLIGENCE SUMMARY

Army Form C. 2118.

(Erase heading not required.)

Place	Date	Hour	Summary of Events and Information	Remarks and references to Appendices
	19.		Getting accommodation available there &	
			in the Ecole de G.H.Q. Modern School.	
	20.		Work on'd a forward overhead route and fitting up	
			of signal office at Advanced G in H.Qrs. H.	
	21.		Office opened at Monceuil.	
			Personnel from Equires moved to Monceuil. H.	
	22.		153 Both signals took over maintenance of road line	
			from Izenettes to Polt H.Qrs. Work commenced on taking	
			this line H.	
	23.		Party of 200 Infantry obtained to dig trench for new	
			to Cap Army H.	
	24.		Work on above continued H.	
	25.		Work commenced on alternative overhead route	
			to Anzia Trunk. Work continued on [?] H.	
26–28			— do —	

Vol 21

War Diary
for
51st (H) Divisional Signal Co. R.E.
from 1st to 31st March 1917

CONFIDENTIAL. Army Form C. 2118.

Nº 214

HIGHLAND DIVISION.

WAR DIARY
or
INTELLIGENCE SUMMARY

(Erase heading not required.)

Instructions regarding War Diaries and Intelligence Summaries are contained in F. S. Regs., Part II. and the Staff Manual respectively. Title Pages will be prepared in manuscript.

March 1917

51st (H) Divil Signal.
C. OB. (F.)

Place	Date	Hour	Summary of Events and Information	Remarks and references to Appendices

Army Form C. 2118.

WAR DIARY
or
INTELLIGENCE SUMMARY

(Erase heading not required.)

March 1917

Place	Date	Hour	Summary of Events and Information	Remarks and references to Appendices
Villers Chatel	1		Work continued on burial posts and an alternative overhead route to Anzin Trench commenced.	
	2-4		Work commenced in fitting up new Signal Offices at Advanced Divisional Hqr.	
	5		Burial posts continued to Bob Hqr.	
	6		Commenced work in burying down forward to Bthu.	
	7-10		Work continued	
	10		Location of Arty O.P.s received. Work commenced in burying down forward from main route to these O.P.s	
	11-16		Work continued as above	
	17		Bde W. A. M. Glasswell from Guards Div. arrived to take over command of Company	

Army Form C. 2118.

WAR DIARY
or
INTELLIGENCE SUMMARY
(Erase heading not required.)

Instructions regarding War Diaries and Intelligence Summaries are contained in F. S. Regs., Part II. and the Staff Manual respectively. Title Pages will be prepared in manuscript.

Place	Date	Hour	Summary of Events and Information	Remarks and references to Appendices
	18-		Capt. Stewell took over command as from 9 am 15th day	
	19-24th		Men Officer opened at YEAN. There was laid to the various O.P.s and Battery positions	
	24		From O.P.s our Infantry were observed as visual signallers work continued.	
	25		Wires laid to Bde Battle H.Q. - D.H. Section carried out experiments with Power buzzers, good results obtained	
	26		Divisional O.P. and Gunners dugout hut in YEAN -	
	27		All lines tested out and faults cleared	
	28		Office at adv. meanwhile occupied by 152 Bde headquarters	
			the Div HQ -	
	29		All cable and other transport from Villers Chatel to	
	30-31		acq. Marquint. Work on forward lines continued	

J. Winter Lt.
51st Signal Co.
(RED)

CONFIDENTIAL.
No.
HIGHLAND DIVISION.

Signals 51
Vol 22

W A R   D I A R Y.

A P R I L   1 9 1 7.

R.E. 51st (Highland) Signal Co.

Army Form C. 2118

WAR DIARY
or
INTELLIGENCE SUMMARY
(Erase heading not required.)

Instructions regarding War Diaries and Intelligence Summaries are contained in F.S. Regs., Part II. and the Staff Manual respectively. Title Pages will be prepared in manuscript.

Place	Date	Hour	Summary of Events and Information	Remarks and references to Appendices
Field	April 1st to 6th		Advanced party of Company at MAROEUIL engaged making a hop pole route and a trestle route from Divisional Hqrs. at Cemetry Maroeuil to Chausse Brunehaut and from there a bury to join the rear end of the Corps bury near ANZIN. Small parties also working in the trenches east of ECURIE and ROCLINCOURT joining the Corp buries and also in laying cables to Battalion Hqrs from Bdes.	
	6th		Company moved to Maroeuil 2/ Corporal Anderson and Sappers R. Ramsay and D. Tod killed at 15½ Battle Hqrs at Roclincourt.	
	7th		Horse lines moved to ACQ.	
	8th		Bdes. moved to their Battle Hqrs.	
	9th		Division attacked. Communication remained good during the whole attack.	
	10, 11th		In/	

1875 Wt. W593/826 1,000,000 4/15 J.B.C. & A. A.D.S.S./Forms/C.2118.

Army Form C. 2118

WAR DIARY
or
INTELLIGENCE SUMMARY

(Erase heading not required.)

Instructions regarding War Diaries and Intelligence Summaries are contained in F. S. Regs., Part II. and the Staff Manual respectively. Title Pages will be prepared in manuscript.

Place	Date	Hour	Summary of Events and Information	Remarks and references to Appendices
	19. 11th		In action. Buried system stood well and Battalion lines were kept through and pushed forward to advanced Batn. Hqrs as these went forward.	S.T
	12th		Moved to HERMAVILLE.	S.T
	13th		Resting.	S.T
	14th		Advance party left for ST. NICHOLAS and a forward party went to Advanced Divisional Hqrs. at the Railway Embankment near ATHIES to lay forward lines	S.T
	15th		Sergt. R. JOLLY killed and Sapper A.R. LEDINGHAM severely wounded at ATHIES. Work commenced in laying lines forward from HERVIN FARM to FAMPOUX	S.T
	16th		Further party left for Hervin Farm to relieve 9th Division.	S.T
	17th - 19th		Three pairs twisted D5 laid over the open and four pairs armoured twin laid in river up to FAMPOUX where exchange was fitted up in cellar of Chateau	S.T

Army Form C. 2118

WAR DIARY
or
INTELLIGENCE SUMMARY

(Erase heading not required.)

Instructions regarding War Diaries and Intelligence Summaries are contained in F. S. Regs., Part II. and the Staff Manual respectively. Title Pages will be prepared in manuscript.

Place	Date	Hour	Summary of Events and Information	Remarks and references to Appendices
			3.	
	20th		Chateau there.	A.T.
	21st		Office opened at ACQ.	D.T.
	22nd		Capt. W.A.M. STAWELL wounded at FAMPOUX. Pnr. W.M. Bray wounded.	A.T.
			Sapper A. R. McDonald wounded.	
			Four pairs run across the open from exchange at FAMPOUX to the two Brigades in action. Bdes. at the same time laying lines to their Btn.	
	23rd		Battle Hqrs.	A.T.
			A shell came through the Signal office at ST.NICHOLAS killing a Corps D.R. and wounding three men (L/Cpl Cox, Spr. J. Michie & Spr. J.A. Rae. 10 motor cycles, 8 push cycles and 7 horses were killed. were destroyed	
			L/Cpl R.D. Robb wounded.	
			Division attacked; lines to Brigades worked well but it was almost impossible to maintain lines form Brigade forward owing to the extreme violence of the enemy shelling and most of the communication was done with/	

1875 Wt. W 593/826 1,000,000 4/15 J.B.C. & A. A.D.S.S./Forms/C. 2118.

WAR DIARY
or
INTELLIGENCE SUMMARY

(Erase heading not required.)

Army Form C. 2118

Place	Date	Hour	Summary of Events and Information	Remarks and references to Appendices
	24th		with the aid of runners. The rear office was moved late in the afternoon to the South African dugout in August Trench near Sunday Avenue. Fighting continued. Lines were maintained and new lines laid from Bdes to Btns.	J.T.
	25th		Company moved to CHELERS on being relieved by 34th Division	J.T.
			Wagon lines to Herlin les Verte	J.T.
	26th		Wagon lines moved from Herlin to Chelers.	J.T.
	27th		Work commenced in clearing lines in Chelers and surrounding villages	J.T.
	28th - 30th		Company resting and refitting.	J.T.

D. Sutherland Capt.
for O.C. 51st (Highland) Divisional
Signal Co.-R.E.-(T)

CONFIDENTIAL

Nº 71(A)

Army Form C. 2118.

WAR DIARY
or
INTELLIGENCE SUMMARY.
(Erase heading not required.)

51 Div Signal Coy

HIGHLAND DIVISION

Vol 23

War Diary
of
May 1917.

51st (H) Divnl Signal Coy (TF)

Place	Date	Hour	Summary of Events and Information	Remarks and references to Appendices

Instructions regarding War Diaries and Intelligence Summaries are contained in F. S. Regs., Part II. and the Staff Manual respectively. Title pages will be prepared in manuscript.

Army Form C. 2118.

WAR DIARY
or
INTELLIGENCE SUMMARY.
(Erase heading not required.)

Instructions regarding War Diaries and Intelligence Summaries are contained in F. S. Regs., Part II. and the Staff Manual respectively. Title pages will be prepared in manuscript.

Place	Date	Hour	Summary of Events and Information	Remarks and references to Appendices
	Feb 9th		Company active and refitting. Headquarters at Etelrus. JF	
	10th		Advance party left for Hermaville. JF	
	11th		Advance party to L.A. Dugouts. Company moved from Etelrus to Hermaville 154 Inf Bde. JF	
	12th		Advance party engaged in bringing cables to local officer at L.A. Dugouts. Moved from PENIN to "Y" Huts & Annex & Pot Road JF	
	13th		Company moved to L.A. Dugouts relieving 4th Div Sapper Coy. Cable sent to Tenpaux and to Cushing to take over forward exchange. JF	
	14th		Wires laid to Ordnance & Anon. 154 Bde moved to Anon. JF	

JF McC Capt RE OC

Army Form C. 2118.

WAR DIARY
or
INTELLIGENCE SUMMARY.
(Erase heading not required.)

Place	Date	Hour	Summary of Events and Information	Remarks and references to Appendices
	15th		Two lines (repaired) to Advanced Dressing Station A.S.N. two M.O. Dump. 1 mule killed and one wounded at Hampour.	
	16th		Four lines during German bombardment were broken during which leaving the need owing to the 5 four being brought in we are in spite of by different routes as we had arranged these cable by another field. Communication was maintained by wireless during famous period. Two were wounded at 152 Bde. 1 man killed + 1 man wounded at 152 Bde. 154 Bde formerly moved two annex to Bdy Endorsement.	
	17th		Four lines repaired + enforced and brought into Hampour Exchange by different routes by 154 returned 132 Bde at the Cutting.	
16th &	19th		Ext 2 fair in Case bury for Cutting N° 24 N B.6.2 and laid there.	

J. Edward Copen R.E. (?)

Army Form C. 2118.

WAR DIARY
or
INTELLIGENCE SUMMARY.
(Erase heading not required.)

Instructions regarding War Diaries and Intelligence Summaries are contained in F. S. Regs., Part II. and the Staff Manual respectively. Title pages will be prepared in manuscript.

Place	Date	Hour	Summary of Events and Information	Remarks and references to Appendices
	20th		Lines of armoured twin to right Bde at H.23.B.3.1 and 1 pair to left Bde at H.16.C.1.6. Owing to lines forward of Bdes being continually broken communication was maintained forward of Bdes by means of visual and power buzzer. A Wireless station was also established at left Bde Hqrs.	
	21st		Permanent route commenced to B.X. trench Mor.	
			Arty. Signalling personnel transferred to OCs.	
	22nd		Work on permanent route completed.	
	23rd		Obtained 2 more turn in Corps being gone on pair to arty. on line to right arty. + from the other laid a line to left Bde at H.16.C.1.6.	
	24th			

J. Bruce Castle ?

WAR DIARY
or
INTELLIGENCE SUMMARY.

Army Form C. 2118.

Place	Date	Hour	Summary of Events and Information	Remarks and references to Appendices
	24.		Two hours to Cobbet Circus. Capt Christie & 2nd M.C. Lieut Gray & Pte. Moffat (Regan away) killed by an explosion in an ammunition dump near 154 Bde Hqrs. M.E. Cpl. Chalmers, wounded. JH	
	25.		Work commenced on relieving old lines around Divl. Hqrs. 88th Bde Hqrs. moved from H.23.B.3.1. to forward & had Hqrs. at Cutting (H.14.a.1.4) forward lines managed owing to change of Bde forward lines becoming 1st Aust. lines. Artillery & Wireless pst moved forward to Rower Wood and trestle through. JH	
	26.		Attempted to trace out some more lines in German keep to North of Ythies but without success. JH	
	27.		Relieving old lines in embankment - 2½ miles of short lengths of D.5. collected & joined, & put on drums. JH	

J.H. Mackay RE

Army Form C. 2118.

WAR DIARY
or
INTELLIGENCE SUMMARY.

(Erase heading not required.)

Instructions regarding War Diaries and Intelligence Summaries are contained in F. S. Regs., Part II. and the Staff Manual respectively. Title pages will be prepared in manuscript.

Place	Date	Hour	Summary of Events and Information	Remarks and references to Appendices
	27th		Hellophones issued to Bns.	
	28th		C.C. Sigs J.K. Irwin went out home with a view to taking and.	
	31st		152 Bde relieved and marched to Arras H.Q.	

Major Caskie (?) former O.C. Stationary Sub Signal C. 25 (?)

2353 Wt. W2544/1454 700,000 5/15 D.D.&L. A.D.S.S./Forms/C. 2118.

Army Form C. 2118.

WAR DIARY
or
INTELLIGENCE SUMMARY.
(Erase heading not required.)

Vol D

War Diary

June 1917.

51st (H) Divnl. Signal Co, R.E. (1)

Army Form C. 2118.

WAR DIARY
or
INTELLIGENCE SUMMARY.
(Erase heading not required.)

Place	Date	Hour	Summary of Events and Information	Remarks and references to Appendices
	4th		All communication to Bates maintained by S/R	S/R
	5th		Headquarters + Nos section moved to Bonny. Advance party of Bonny for Gorophki 15th Bde. left. Returned. Failure of Wireless	S/R
	6th		Resting at Bonny	S/R
	7th		Company moved to Afrikanius. Signal Office established at Morris. 15th Bde Wh Newton proceeded to Mardanique.	S/R
	8		Wire laid to local office & to 15th Bde 15th Bde Wire lines to Bde Party returned unit from Garophette	S/R

2353 Wt. W3544/1454 700,000 5/15 D.D.&L. A.D.S.S./Forms/C. 2118.

WAR DIARY
or
INTELLIGENCE SUMMARY.

(Erase heading not required.)

Army Form C. 2118.

Place	Date	Hour	Summary of Events and Information	Remarks and references to Appendices
Field	1st April		Advance party left 3rd Division for Pollacourt. 9th Divn. 2nd Armies are [proceeded] to Pollacourt.	DJ
	2nd		Captn. Marsden B. Pollacourt on being relieved by 9th Divn. C.C. Col. Sober joined Hqrs: pro communication established with 152 Bde.	DJ
	3rd		A sub-section from 39th Nuclear Sobre joined unit.	DJ
	4th		Capt Spear transferred 2nd Army Signal School. Capt. (?) Sutherland became 2nd in Command. Advance party left for Chedegnies. Company moved to Perne. 152 Bde left Pollacourt & proceeded to Artignard Chateau	DJ

ally

WAR DIARY
or
INTELLIGENCE SUMMARY.

Army Form C. 2118.

Place	Date	Hour	Summary of Events and Information	Remarks and references to Appendices
	21st Sept		Corps Cadre Riding & Rifting at Etaples officers Classes commenced in visual Signalling & Buzzer. Classes commenced in Code School. Cape school commenced	D.1
	22nd		15th Bde moved to Tincourdinghe	D.1
	22nd		117 M.T. Coy, 39th Divn lent out for the 4th order of the 8th Cav head qrs of the 29th Divn to form part of the Anonendices. Coy H.Q. moved to Lederzule. Divn. said to have officer	D.1
	23rd-30th		Training in classes continued	D.1

J. Rutherford Col
AA G5.7A(A) & rd Signal
(88C)

Army Form C. 2118.

Vol 25

WAR DIARY
or
INTELLIGENCE SUMMARY.
(Erase heading not required.)

War Diary
July 1917

57th M. Amb. Cy. C.D.S.t

Army Form C. 2118.

WAR DIARY
or
INTELLIGENCE SUMMARY.
(Erase heading not required.)

Instructions regarding War Diaries and Intelligence Summaries are contained in F. S. Regs., Part II and the Staff Manual respectively. Title pages will be prepared in manuscript.

Place	Date	Hour	Summary of Events and Information	Remarks and references to Appendices
Hilo	July	1st	Party Section left for "X" Camp. Remained at E. at Zillebeke. Class continued as usual. and card drill.	J.S.
		2nd	Rop pole route made to Nieuwpoort — Visual classes cont. 152 kobi at 9.5. Nieuwpoort.	J.S.
		3rd	"O.O." Cable Section left for "X" Camp.	J.S.
		4th	En half + Headquarters packing sect. left for "X" Camp. C.O.'s cable section opened Hd Cof. — Rode over from 153 bde. moved to a 30 Central. 152 bde.	J.S.
		5th to 6th	Small advance party to Canal Bank leaving behind reception and establishing advanced Div. Sig. Office	J.S.

2353 Wt. W2344/1454 700,000 5/15 D, D, & L. A.D.S.S./Forms/C. 2118.

Army Form C. 2118.

WAR DIARY
or
INTELLIGENCE SUMMARY.
(Erase heading not required.)

Instructions regarding War Diaries and Intelligence Summaries are contained in F.S. Regs., Part II. and the Staff Manual respectively. Title pages will be prepared in manuscript.

Place	Date	Hour	Summary of Events and Information	Remarks and references to Appendices
	9th		"Y.1" force action attacked for duty. Pioneer Gr. A. Stephen killed. Pioneer System robe. Regime from Highland travel to Lancashire travel. Work as above continued.	JS
	10th	8am-9pm		JS
		am.	Not commenced an incompleted turns from Lancashire down the Willows and from Willows to 200h Evan. 9th Seton left Nulnelinghe & entrained at St Omer de. arrived at Pofpringhe and marched to "B" camp (A.30 Central) 152 Bole relieved in the line by 154 Bole	JS
	11th		Work as above could 152 Bole entrained at Pofpringhe and entrained at St Omer and proceeded by road to Katerzeele.	JS

2353 Wt. W3141/1454 700,000 5/15 D.D.&L. A.D.S.S./Forms/C. 2118.

Army Form C. 2118.

WAR DIARY
or
INTELLIGENCE SUMMARY.
(Erase heading not required.)

Instructions regarding War Diaries and Intelligence Summaries are contained in F. S. Regs., Part II. and the Staff Manual respectively. Title pages will be prepared in manuscript.

Place	Date	Hour	Summary of Events and Information	Remarks and references to Appendices
	12th		Buried Route from Highland to Lancashire. Buried Route from Lancashire to Wiltons etc took from finished end into dugouts at Wiltons and Stock.	J.S.
	13th		Highland to Lancashire and Lancashire to Wiltons and Stock nosked and put on terminal strips at each end.	J.S.
	14th		Local lines from armoured Signal Office to huts along Canal Bank begun. Armoured Cable dump found at Bridge 4 and carts sent up.	J.S.
	15th TO 17th		Local lines continued, found ropes of three lane each twisted to 5 led by different routes from armoured dugout Office to around each Coy. Army at R. dugout.	J.S.

Army Form C. 2118.

WAR DIARY
or
INTELLIGENCE SUMMARY.

(Erase heading not required.)

Instructions regarding War Diaries and Intelligence Summaries are contained in F.S. Regs., Part II. and the Staff Manual respectively. Title pages will be prepared in manuscript.

Place	Date	Hour	Summary of Events and Information	Remarks and references to Appendices
	17th		152 Bn. Practice attack at Gr. Moncler	J.T.
	18th to 20th		Bns. on rest carried out visual schemes on training ground.	J.T.
	20th		152, & 153rd Bns. carry out practice attacks. Sections carried out signalling schemes in accordance with S.S. 148.	J.T.
	21st.		Signal Officer rejoining & testing lines and attaining breaks on buried system.	J.T.
	22nd.		Lt. T. M. Cumming (4/5 Seaforth Hrs.) took over Mobile Section	D.T.
	23rd			

2353 Wt. W2544/1454 700,000 5/15 D.D.& L. A.D.S.S./Forms/C. 2118.

WAR DIARY
or
INTELLIGENCE SUMMARY.
(Erase heading not required.)

Army Form C. 2118.

Instructions regarding War Diaries and Intelligence Summaries are contained in F. S. Regs., Part II. and the Staff Manual respectively. Title pages will be prepared in manuscript.

Place	Date	Hour	Summary of Events and Information	Remarks and references to Appendices
	23rd		T/Lt J.N. Laird admitted to hospital. T/Lt Gunning with advance party left Sidi-gul-Ighil to Camp	
	24th		152 Bde moves into "B" Camp advance party to Sadi Harin (Sidi Abpu)	
	25th		Highland & Lancashire Terr. Horse burst by artillery fire and repaired.	
	27th		Work on R.R.a damaged by Labour Bn making new road.	
	28th		152 Bde moved into line (Hope Rock Farm) Three lines overland cable laid from Advanced Signal Office to E.T. on main busy Road.	
	30th			

Army Form C. 2118.

WAR DIARY
or
INTELLIGENCE SUMMARY.
(Erase heading not required.)

Place	Date	Hour	Summary of Events and Information	Remarks and references to Appendices
	8/8/17		Lines put through to advanced Boch. Hqs. Advanced Boch dumps found at Pot. Hqs and lines moved through to Bob. B. Rec. laid from D3 cable to each of the two Bn Hqrs in British front line. Capt J. Spence M.C. came with.	D.1
	2/8/17		3rd Battle of YPRES. Commenced at 3.50 pm. No communication with all Bns forward pns. by phone visual runners & pigeons. Owing to bad weather contact aeroplane by wireless was useless. Wireless Amplifiers & Power Buzzers did not work satisfactorily.	D.1

D Sutherland Capt / in C. 5 7 (A.A) Divie Sig Co RE.

Vol. 26

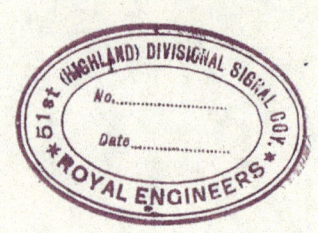

CONFIDENTIAL

WAR DIARY
OF
51st [HIGHLAND] DIVISIONAL
SIGNAL COMPANY
RE. T.F.

from 1st AUGUST 1917 to
31st AUGUST 1917

J Muirhead
Maj RE
OC 51 Sig Coy RE

37th Signal Company

Army Form C. 2118.

August 1917

WAR DIARY
or
INTELLIGENCE SUMMARY.
(Erase heading not required.)

Instructions regarding War Diaries and Intelligence Summaries are contained in F. S. Regs., Part II. and the Staff Manual respectively. Title pages will be prepared in manuscript.

Place	Date	Hour	Summary of Events and Information	Remarks and references to Appendices
Camp	1st	5.15	Capt (A/Major) James Stevenson took over command of Company.	
	2nd	10.00	Capt (A/Major) J. Lupwood RE left company. Proceeded to 2nd Army. Capt Stevens RE OC Company to inspect 3rd Army School.	
			132 Bn take over Div Hdrs. Sent 9/0 L.Cpl Farrar wireless station at Wormhoudt farm discharged hostile wireless. G Control generally normal.	
	3rd		Bernard went to forward N.land encampment. New road from YPRES to F.Wyrd. suggested & photographs. He arrived to fit head of depot at Divison.	
	4th		Capt Stevenson returned forward area for German burst again. Nothing heard.	
	5		Remainder of Company again on fatigues. Above T SPS depot commenced.	
	6-7		- do -	
			9 RE depot	
			"	
			44 metres of cable laid in military funnel	

Instructions regarding War Diaries and Intelligence Summaries are contained in F. S. Regs., Part II. and the Staff Manual respectively. Title pages will be prepared in manuscript.

WAR DIARY
or
INTELLIGENCE SUMMARY.
(Erase heading not required.)

Army Form C. 2118.

Place	Date	Hour	Summary of Events and Information	Remarks and references to Appendices
	8		Div headquarters move to [illegible]	
	9.		Overhaul stores & equipment.	
	10		154 Bde move to [illegible]. 70 Bde occupy camp vacated by them and are connected to Div Exchange.	
	11		10 men from 153 Bde send to 8th Corps school for instruction in Power buzzer & amplifier. Linesmen class begun at Div Hdqrs.	
	12 to 16	}	Riding school and linesmen classes of Company begun & continued	
	16		8 linesmen sent to 5 Cps school.	
	17		Classes continued. Cpl Low granted bar to MM. Sgt [illegible] & Cpl [illegible] granted MM.	
	18		Div Hdqrs move to [illegible].	
	19.		12 men send to wireless course at 5th Corps School.	
	20 to		Classes continued	
	22		Capt [illegible] reported to take command of Company	
	23.		Capt (A/Major) F [illegible] proceeds to hospital. Capt [illegible] takes command of Company.	

Army Form C. 2118.

WAR DIARY
or
INTELLIGENCE SUMMARY.
(Erase heading not required.)

Instructions regarding War Diaries and Intelligence Summaries are contained in F. S. Regs., Part II. and the Staff Manual respectively. Title pages will be prepared in manuscript.

Place	Date	Hour	Summary of Events and Information	Remarks and references to Appendices
ASRM HOOT.	23/8/17		Training :- 1 Pet N° 1 Section cable layg, Buzzer, Visual & Lucas train to HQ & N° 1. Div Section in Pigeons, Visual, Lineman's Drill, P.A. & amplifier. Sgt Napier awarded Military Medal for gallantry (XIII Corps A 458)	App
	24/8/17		Training as above. Visit to ABD Signals.	
	25/6/17		Corps G. II Div Signals Situation unchanged. Bugs:	
	26/8/17		Bombs requisitioned to Canal Trench & CC & Capt's Sutherland. G. VIII Cops to Bois Bugger course. Capt Sutherland & 2/CCS continue E. of canal bank. Inspection of say R, & of horses & wagons. Report & communicate forward to G staff.	
	27/8/17		Arrangements of taking over emplates.	
	28/8/17		20 Linesmen sent to Canal Bank, 2 Li Bridge camp. 2 instrument repairers to Dr Sch camp. All technical stores sent to Bridge camp. Are written also will 8 works personnel & 90 fitters sent to Canal Bank. 152 Bde Sigs L. J. on final lines. O.C. Capt. Bruce & Lieut Fair next 11 Div Signals at Canal Bank & Bridge Camp. Arrangements made in take over officers :- vs all bat personnel obtained uniy to the left, all writers large nets in via to be left in line & operators taken over. 6 SDS borrowed for Capt to replace the of V Carp wireless wrote lost wales (TV section) instructs delay line to MURAT CAMP & 174 Bde. Nm Exchange installed. JBrix Camp	
BRIDGE CAMP	29/8/17		Div HQ note to Broder Camp at 2 pm. Coy move by road. Signal office there taken over from 11th Div. 152 Bde take over line. 154 move to Munat Camp. 153 remain at St Taro & Burger. Staff & road line run. 11 Div Sigs in command of front, and functioning at Canal Bank.	

51st SIGNAL COMPANY RE

WAR DIARY or INTELLIGENCE SUMMARY

AUGUST 1917. Army Form C. 2118.

Place	Date	Hour	Summary of Events and Information	Remarks and references to Appendices
BUDDEN CAMP	30/8/17		51 Div took over command of front at 11 a.m. 152 Bde in line at CANE POST. 154 Bde at TROIS TOURS CH.=s; 153 Bde move fm ST JANS TER BIEZEN to SIEGE CAMP. Dumps Rd at No 3 section at Siege Camp hit & destroyed by HV gun - no casualties. Div Sig. Office opened at CANAL BANK & telephone from CANAL BANK to 752 P.S, no superimposed. 4 p.m. 51 Div to CANAL BANK are superimposed. 153 & 154 Bde work superimposed. Div Cable exchange at DivHQrs & CANAL BANK. F.A. Bde wires between them. Cpl. SILLARS with Lieut McLaren & Kemp at Adv. Office, remain to take over test dugouts for 115 Div signals. Div agree to provide infant patrols to complete lines to HURST PARK & SW Regnt. Visited Bdes in rest. Div advanced office. Cap. Sgermain, Signals, DR's Wisdom, etc arranged.	
	31/8/17		Visited PFA Bde & D.C. stores. Infants parties arranged & work details. High Command & Cane Trench renewed, working lamp. Amplifier at HANNIX PKK for withdrawal, as Bath HQ moves back. Personnel & instrument kept in reserve. Arranged with 153 Bde Cph. they will obtain Sigal Officer from Battns to go to a course with XVIII Corps, HQ Signal accept to Gen. arrange for training of 2 officers for wireless. Lattigis Batts with 153 Bde Cable Dumps late at Canal Bank & Minty Farm. A good Cadoeti reserve of Cable is behind Div HQrs. Lines starting weak & communication not interrupted.	J Mauchen Major RE Comd, 51 Sigal Coy

51st DIVISIONAL SIGNALS

APPENDIX I.

NOTES on AREA to be taken over from 11th Div.

GENERAL:- Up to the Canal Bank Corps overhead routes now supplement the original lines, & no difficulty is anticipated in this area.

CANAL BANK - CANE TRENCH: Owing to heavy shelling last week lines are somewhat chaotic, but not much should be required to make this area sound. From the ends of the old buried system ditched routes with several lateral connections run from Lancashire Farm to Cane Trench & High Command to Trinity Farm respectively. Several small additional ditches & ground routes supplement these.

CANE TRENCH - forward:- Above 2 routes are carried forward across the STEENBECK to C5a 2.8 & Bulgar Farm respectively. These are partly ditched & partly ground cable, & were successfully maintained. Test stations in "pill boxes" are maintained every few hundred yards. These routes with one or two ground lines in addition provide Brigade to Battalion lines, & one OP line to each RFA Brigade.

WORK PROPOSED:-

Communication to CANE TRENCH would be strengthened if wires could be laid in CALABASH AVENUE & CALEDONIA TRENCH & these trenches filled in above them. A deep bury should be dug from about C14c 6.6 to C14b 3.5 connecting the end of the old bury with CALABASH AVENUE. It is estimated that this work would take 1000 man days, & could be done in daylight in dull weather. Bury would need camouflaging by battery positions.

Forward routes will be continued as far forward as possible. Attempts to ditch these routes have proved of doubtful value, as anything in the nature of a marked trench has drawn fire & spread out lines dug in at crossing places etc have stood better. Further experience may show this conclusion to be wrong. It is impossible to dig any depth in the Steenbeck Valley.

Remaining work is of a technical nature (see below) & labour is not required meantime. One cable section from 5 Corps Signal Coy will assist the Divisional Coy. The Brigade à line will receive similar assistance from the Division.

COMMUNICATIONS to be ESTABLISHED

2.

COMMUNICATIONS to be Established:-

DIV. EXCHANGE at Border Camp will be connected to:-

XVIII Corps	Div. Arty. Exchange
XVIII Corps H.A.	Div Adv. Exchange (Canal Bank)
Flank Divisions	Pigeon Loft
152 Bde	Div. Train
153 Bde	& Staff Offices
154 Bde	

DIV ADVANCED EXCHANGE (CANAL BANK) will be connected to:-

152 Bde	Div Visual Station (High Command Redoubt)
Foch Farm Exch. (for 152 Bde)	Field Coys
Corps Wireless Directg Station	Flank Adv. Divisions
Div Exch.	

DIV. R.A. EXCHANGE:-

Main Exchange will be at Canal Bank, a small office only being run at Div HQs. for the CRA. At present R.A. Exch. is on the E. side of the canal, but it will be moved as soon as possible to the same spot as Div Adv. Exch. to facilitate working.

This Exchange will have direct communication to all RA Bdes etc.

TELEGRAPH SYSTEM.

Telegraph will be worked from Div HQs to:-

- XVIII Corps
- 153 Bde
- 154 Bde.
- Div Adv. (transit to RA Bdes).
- Foch Farm (transit to 152 Bde).

If possible direct telegraph will be worked to 152 Bde, but at present lines will not admit of this. It should be possible to remedy this.

Diagrams of above.

Telephone Trunks:-

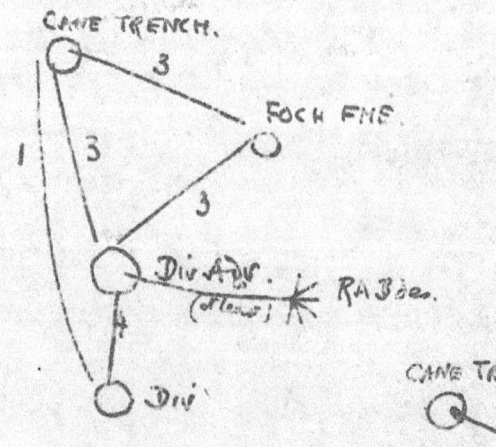

Telegraph.

3/

WIRELESS:-
D.S. is at Canal Bank & is connected by telephone to Div Hdr.
It works to Div. Set at CANE TRENCH.
This set works to RED HOUSE.
Power Buzzers & Amplifiers giving communication forward & back are
at   CANE TRENCH
       BULGAR FME
       HANNIXBECK FME.

(Hannixbeck   A∅
 Fme)   \
                 \   W (Red House)
                  \
                   \   A∅ (Bulgar Fme)
                    \
          A∅ W. Cane Trench
                      \
                       \
                        \
                         \
                          \
                           \
                            W. Canal Bank

VISUAL.
Div Station is at High Command Redoubt:-
It works to CANE TRENCH & to Canal Bank.
Cane Trench can obtain all Bttns & Corps direct.

PIGEONS:- About 16 pairs per diem are available. These are sent by Corps to Irish Farm and drawn there by D.R.

DOGS:- 6 dogs live at Canal bank. These have given good results for front line.

DRLS:- It will be impossible to count on motorcyclists E. of canal bank, tho' in dry weather & when roads are clear a cyclist might reach Foch Fme eg.
It will be necessary to obtain mounted orderlies to the number of 4 at least to relay from Canal Bank to Foch Fme. These should live at Foch Farm as at present.
Runners from Foch Farm to Cane Trench are required. Bns. ont. line might supply these. 6 are needed as a minimum.

GERMAN CABLES:-
These have been noted at various points. An officer will be detailed to investigate. Could Corps Intelligence provide any maps obtained from air photographs before the advance?

4)

Communications are bound to be difficult as the ground affords no protection in case of heavy shelling. Speech to Cave Trench fm Div. HQs will always be precarious as the original buried cables are faulty, & it may not be possible to cure this; while other routes are at the mercy of a chance shell.

J. Muirhead
Capt. RE
O. Signals 51st Division.

27/8/17

CONFIDENTIAL.
No 21 A
HIGHLAND
DIVISION.

Vol 27

CONFIDENTIAL.

WAR DIARY

OF

51st (HIGHLAND) SIGNAL

COMPANY R.E. T.F.

from   to
  Septbr   Septbr
1st ~~August~~ 1917   30th ~~August~~ 1917.

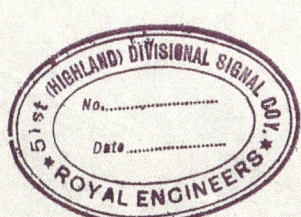

JMuirhead
Major RE
Comdg.

51st SIGNAL COMPANY
R.E.

WAR DIARY or INTELLIGENCE SUMMARY

Army Form C.2118.

SEPTEMBER 1917
Sheet 1.

Place	Date	Hour	Summary of Events and Information	Remarks and references to Appendices
BORDER CAMP.	1st Sept 1917		Infantry party of 50 men complete burying (84 pairs) to CW Test joint (C28 NW2 15a & 65). Reconnoitred of lines – Yr to F (C25 a 7.4) to Fork Farm. Result depends upon & improved. Canal Bank cleared up of duplicates & non-strugglers. Canal Bank office renum's, and as Fort Farm test point. Clearing up Duck Camp. OC visits all test points & workparties up to Div. Town Duges & Amplifier moved for HANNIXBEEK FARM to Left Battn HQrs. Wagon to Fabricius Farm. Bombed at night – no lives lost.	
"	2nd Sept 1917		OC visits Bn test points & battalion in line, & visited new forward cable. Teams sent to be ready from Poelstraat to Fabricius Farm. Maintenance of lines steady. At M 12, 50 men digging open buried CW towards Minty Farm. To replace scattered cable. Bombing at night – no lives lost.	
"	3rd Sept	10.30 am	Heavy shelling. All telephone communication down to 152 B.Br. Srounbn still working. Visual standpipes by Hindenburg Farm. & route OK. but speed to pairs to use. Whizbk put on lift route on standby. 11.15. OK again. Centurions shelling of area from in front of HQ Command to Fordie Farm. Lines continually broken, but communication kept thro' by amphibs. Working party carrying hand toward Minty Farm. – party caught in barrage returning – 2 infanty killed. Burial Forde Farm to Bgr & Bgr to CW Cat. Bombing at night. Visual station at HQ Command knocked out – all material destroyed – personnel unhurt.	
4th Sept. 5th Sep.			Buried lines repaired. Maintenance of lines. Shelling bombs near Div area. Communication maintained. Ditzl cripts between Park maintenance. SFHs and 15 Hmst Park on platoon, 8 pairs. Cleaning up Duck Camp. Sleep trenches & tackaways.	

Army Form C. 2118.

51st SIGNAL COY RE WAR DIARY or INTELLIGENCE SUMMARY.

SEPTEMBER 1917
Sheet 2.

(Erase heading not required.)

Place	Date	Hour	Summary of Events and Information	Remarks and references to Appendices
BORDER CAMP.	6/9/17		Route to HURST PARK put into use. Maintenance. Conference of all Sigal officers of Division re protection of wires. Raid by 152 Bde. All communication found & Battalion's out. No report of raid forthcoming except on pigeon message. German attack on XIX Corps & Second Army front in afternoon detaching us no other Div in area. Enemy Quiet night. Party clean-up area.	
	7/9/17		154 Div relieve 152 Bde in line. 7a.m. Maintenance, cleaning up area. Moral Corps shelled by early morn, no wires lines broken. A.D. Signals asked to take in hand remaining stats units Y.P & F. Bombs at night and during s. Usual heavy shellfire into Div area - Long Ldd, HiLLs 3RD & Wire cuts recommitted from Bde to Sketchbook nil. Came across Saneen Morris Farm & Lt. Scheren to communications units & staff to prepare schemes. Lecture on Fullaphone to 152 Bde Sigals.	
	8/9/17		Quiet day. 11.30 am 154 Bde Sigal office directly hit. Spr Whyte & Henman wound, Office wrecked. Office transferred to LD last point temporarily & communication reestablished 11.45 pm. Some shelling forward. Parties arranged for Bury & STEENBECK. Route Tapes out. Visited 154 Bde - Sigal office established in dugout about 50 yards from wrecked one. Good deal of shelling between old line & Canal Bury YP to F traffic Barrages, & miles to be cut. Maintenance. Heavy shelling at night between H.Q. Geneva & Cana Park, & round Stock Farm. All wires cut at various times. Fullaphone class last & yap for 2nd Div of 153 Bde commenced.	
	9/9/17			
	10/9/17.			
	11/9/17		Pigeon Lecture to 152 Bde. Maintenance. Party of 400 men of 152 Bde digging new Buried PUDERING FRONT to FRANCOISE FARM. AM & YP Cable Sections ready. Parties with drinks Kemp & Co. Geo shelling of area around Bde H.Qs.	

2353 Wt. W2544/1454 700,000 5/15 D. D. & L.   A.D.S.S./Forms/C. 2118.

51st SIGNAL CORPS. September 1917 Army Form C. 2118.

WAR DIARY
or
INTELLIGENCE SUMMARY.
(Erase heading not required.)

Sheet 3

Place	Date	Hour	Summary of Events and Information	Remarks and references to Appendices
BORDER CAMP	12/9/17		Maintenance. Route CW to LD taped out. Party of 4 for men continue burial cable FRANCOIS FARM towards FERDINAND FARM. Bde HQ's heavily shelled 11-12 noon & 1-2 p.m. Lines stand.	
	13/9/17		Visited part of to Steenbeck & inspected burial. Bury completed to within 1/4 mile of FERDINAND. 400 yards of bury dug by day fm CW towards CANE POST – 24 pair pulled in. Amplifier withdrawn fm Battn HQ & not personal overhead system. 153 Bde relieved 154 Bde at about 7:00 am. Lieut MacEwing of Staff, went South on 7 days leave.	
	14/9/17		Scheme of Brigade communication discussed with Bde & Bn Staff of 154 Bde. Maintenance. Burial completed to within 100 yards of LD & Ferdinand Farm.	
	15/9/17		Maintenance. Visited area up to Steenbek. Work on burial continued. Demonstration of Power Buzzer & amplifier to 152 & 154 Bde.	
	16/9/17		Maintenance. Bury completed thro'out fm CW to Jackies Farm. Prelim fm CW to CANE POST taken through – all transfered. Test pit fitted up 150 yds E of HINDENBURG FARM. Pair put thro' & re-gains cde. & tested.	
	17/9/17		Maintenance. New bury cut at joints near Cane Post, where 1 yard has been left unfilled – Visited over poles & walks on line to Steenbek. Proposals for coming operation settled. Work taking bury towards of CANE POST. Test pair's fitted up at RUDOLPHE FARM (FW) FRANCOIS FARM (FU) RUDOLPHE (EW) 1/2 way between CANE POST & RUDOLPHE (SW) 1/2 way between FRANCOIS & FERDINAND (HW) & FERDINAND. Lines taken through RUDOLPHE – FERDINAND – all clear. 20 pair bury in LD to CANE POST office.	

51/2 (HD) SIGNAL COMPANY   September
R.E.T.F   WAR DIARY   1917   Sheet 4
     or
INTELLIGENCE SUMMARY.

Army Form C. 2118.

Place	Date	Hour	Summary of Events and Information	Remarks and references to Appendices
BOESINGHE CAMP	17/9/17		Buried Cables and Completed from Cane Post to Ferdinand Farm. Vanguard lines Langemarck & Burnside. Circuits put through = 253 & 255 Bde I.F.A. to 153 Inf. Bde. Jap. Div. R.A. 2nd to Inf. Bde. Cane Post to Ferdinand Fm. Battalions, 2 pairs to Heavy Artillery O.P's laid through to Ferdinand Farm. Sandbagging of manholes, burying of surplus wires of Cane Post completed. 6 R.F.A. O.P's across the Steenbeck put through to bury as [illegible]. Controls re-laid by R.F.A. Pigeon arrange = 64 way, hot spots, 20 to Tanks, 4 to R.F.A. Cable sent up as follows - to 154 Bde Le Ferrière Farm, to Elphrir to Rat House, to R.H.Q. 10 to Bulow Farm. Amplifier wires Buzzer and 4 valve set with 2 windows, a single & amplifier. In billets at U 29 d 7.6, a 2 valve buzzer to Battalions. Set put through away to shelling. 154 Bde Signals laying 3 pairs from Ferrière farm to R.H.Q. & left Battn H.Q. (Rat House to Bulow Farm). Gotthilon of Phanden arrived, he is going to remain of the Coy Post Office.	
	18/9/17		154 Bde Signals forward of the Post. 154 Bde succeed in laying 3 circuits each up towards left & Reyt Battns so far on Langemarck road. Unable to go further forward owing to damage will continue tonight.	
	19/9/17		Circuits put through to Intelligence Officers of Gournier Rudolphe & Minty Earth, 2 pairs through Duster to Bde, 1 pair. Div. R.A. Arty to Bde. 154 Bde relieve 153. 3 circuits each laid to Rat House - Bulow Farm.	
	20/9/17	5-40am	154 Bde attack Langemarck - Hubercolt line, with 66th Bde on left, 174 on right. Bde Div lines good. 154 Bde - line O.K. to 2 right Battns, down to 2 left. Power Buzzer & amplifier station at U 29 d 7.6 working, message being sent this way.	

51st (H'land) Sig'nal Co'y RE
T.F.

September 1917

WAR DIARY
or
INTELLIGENCE SUMMARY.   Sheet No 5
(Erase heading not required.)

Army Form C. 2118.

Place	Date	Hour	Summary of Events and Information	Remarks and references to Appendices
Border Camp	26/9/17	7.22 am	1st pigeon in - released 6.45am at BULOW FARM	
		12 noon	Situation :- All objectives gained & consolidation proceeding. Signals all in aust to Steenbeek maintained, forward pigeons very good, 20 more birds sent up to Sinai Farm lines through double battalion HQrs but frequently cut. Valuable information received while lines standing, Post Buzzer Through received up to 7.0 am from U29 c 7.6, later Divr.	
			2 Divr circuit put thro' Bespoke Amp to Canepost (YEP - 20D) superimposed.	
		4.30	Enemy counterattacking. All lines down. 7th Power Buzzer th'd 4 pair terminals. Counterattacks answered, div'n thro' to Div. Wireless personnel at forward amplifier covered in rapidly to counterattack.	
			All lines held th'g't battle as far as Steenbeek	
	21/9/17		Visits forward to H.Q. 2 Bde., 2 June thence to each Bde-Sn. Forward Farm. Marcel Fm & 2 Corps.	
			Quiet day - all lines good. Trials amplifying a few buzzers witnessed as accumulators etc gathering & cleaning.	
	22/9/17		Quiet day in back areas. Maintenance. 152 Bde take over during night 21/22 from 154 Bde. Great difficulty will forward lines owing to heavy shelling. Take Farm dugout hut entrance blown in. All lines bridged.	
	23/9/17		Maintenance. Busy cct near Kleine Farm by Divist HQr. Quiet in front areas otherwise. Very heavy shelling at times forward & lines to Bdes frequently cut.	
	24/9/17		Maintenance. 112th Div personnel take over test dugout & forward office. All lines intact thro' to Divs & to Bdes but frequently cut.	
			[illegible] through cable 59t Buzzer relieved 152 Bde Buzzer by 191 All Div instruments to be audited	

51st (Highland) Sigl
Coy RE TF

August 1917
Sheet 6

Army Form C. 2118.

WAR DIARY
or
INTELLIGENCE SUMMARY.
(Erase heading not required.)

Place	Date	Hour	Summary of Events and Information	Remarks and references to Appendices
BOVES Camp	25/9/17		Div HQ. closed at BOVES camp 9.30am & moved off first to such under to 11th Division. Div orders W87/110/T	
WORTHUYST	26/9/17		Signal Company paraded by road to WORTHUYST	
Do	27/9/17		Reorganisation of Lines Sect. & No. 1 Section. Work on Battery & HQ cms	
Do	28/9/17		Packing up & moving fully loaded, road G. ACHIET LE PETIT	
Do	29/9/17		Ditto close at WARTH, forward Hd. to ACHIET LE PETIT & J.W. John Coy	
			moved to PRIMES entrains	
ACHIET LE PETIT	30/9/17		Cy arrived BAPAUME & passed to BOISLEUX AU MONT where to entrain	
			Cy GREEN got Div. HQ starting gear to billeting area & GOC XVIII Corps to	
			allocating the Rd. in 29th Sept 1917	
			(Sd) M. Mentagne	
			Major RE	
			Comg 51st Sigl Coy RE	

No.	G/A 21
To see and initial, please.	

G.O.C.	
G.S.O.1	O C Signals
G.S.O.2	to see &
G.S.O.3 ...JP.Re	return please
I.O.	JP.
"Q"	
C.R.A.	Seen
C.R.E.	LA

Action.-

SECRET.

G.S. 21.
16.10.17.

XVIII Corps No. G.S. 66/252.

1st Division.
9th Division.
32nd Division.

    The attached report on the communications of the 51st Division during operations on September 20th is issued for information.   Attention is specially drawn to para 3.

16th October, 1917.   General Staff, XVIII Corps.

51st (HIGHLAND) DIVISIONAL SIGNAL COMPANY.

Reference Maps -
    ST. JULIEN 28 N.W.2. 1/10,000
    POEL-CAPPELLE Ed. 3. 1/10,000.

Report on communications East of YSER CANAL during the attack of the 20th Sept., 1917.

The area can be conveniently divided into the following:-

    (1) From Divisional Headquarters to the STEENBEEK

    (2) East of the STEENBEEK.

1.   Divisional, Infantry and R.F.A. Brigade Headquarters, and R.F.A. Batteries were all in this area.

No difficulty was experienced in maintaining communications between these formations. Lines were grouped in main buried and trenched routes and were controlled by the Divisional Signal Company from a Forward Exchange and test point in the Canal Bank. One main buried route of 24 pairs was previously dug as far as FERDINAND FARM, and was manned throughout by men of the Divisional Signal Company, 4 signallers from each R.F.A. Brigade being attached in addition. Two trenched routes were also constructed and maintained as far as the line of CANE TRENCH.

Alternate routes were provided in all cases, and speech throughout was excellent.

The system of attaching R.F.A. personnel to the Signal Company thoroughly justified itself, and should be made a permanent arrangement where any buried scheme exists. Relief of the men was left to the R.F.A. Brigades and was satisfactorily arranged.

One liaison line was provided from the Divisional R.A. Adv. Exchange to the attacking Brigade and one from each Artillery Group to the attacking Brigade. This is a satisfactory arrangement and will in future be the standard to be aimed at.

2.   (a) Communication East of the STEENBEEK comprised the following:-
    (i) Communication of attacking Infantry Brigade.
    (ii) Artillery Group observation lines.

Previous to the attack no lines existed East of PARTRIDGE HOUSE and BULGARE FARM.

    (b) It was anticipated that the hostile barrage would be on the line of the STEENBEEK and the LANGEMARCK Road; that communication forward of this area would be comparatively easy, but that great difficulty would be experienced in the area itself.

These anticipations proved correct. To meet the situation the following measures were taken.

    (i) A power buzzer and amplifier were to be established on the night of the 18th in SNIPE HOUSE (U.29.d.7.6) and a power buzzer to be established at BULOW Farm; these stations to work across the barraged area to RED HOUSE.

    (ii) Dumps of cable for Battalion lines were to be formed East of the Barrage line at RAT HOUSE and BULOW FARM on the night of the 18th September.

- 2 -

(iii) 3 circuits each were to be run on the night of the 18th from FERDINAND FARM (end of the bury) to SNIPE HOUSE and BULOW FARM, giving communication between attacking Brigade and its Battalion.

To assist in maintaining these lines 8 Battalion signallers were attached to 154th Brigade Signal Section and the Brigade Section was relieved of all responsibility for the Sector from Brigade Headquarters to FERDINAND FARM. Two officers and linesmen of the Divisional Signal Company were specially detailed to look after this area.

R.F.A., F.O.O's. Circuits were allotted as far as the STEENBEEK for Artillery F.O.O's. the R.F.A. undertaking to continue these lines across the LANGEMARCK ROAD.

(iv) 40 Pigeons were allotted to the attacking Infantry and 24 message carrying rockets.

20 pigeons were allotted to Tanks and 4 to the Artillery.

(v) At a conference of Infantry Signalling Officers and O.C. Signals, it was laid down that after ZERO, forward Signal Stations should be established at PHEASANT FARM and NEW HOUSES and 2 circuits from Battalion Headquarters run to these points by Battalion Signallers of the first two attacking Battalions. If possible the second two battalions would continue these lines towards ROSE HOUSE and FLORA COTTAGE.

Personnel and stores for these parties were detailed by O.C. Signals, and it was arranged that if possible power buzzers should be taken forward and established at PHEASANT FARM and NEW HOUSES.

(vi) By provision for visual signalling and a supply of rockets.

(c) In the event the results of these measures were as follows:-

(i) The central amplifier station was successfully conveyed forward under Divisional arrangements on the night of the 18th. Owing to the heavy barrage, however, it was not until the night of the 19th at 10.30 p.m. that communication was established. The station was working until 9 a.m. on the 20th during which time 12 messages were sent and received. At 9 a.m. the apparatus was put out of action by a shell, and was withdrawn on the night of the 20th to BULGARE FARM.

(ii) Cable dumps were successfully formed, and cable wound on small hand drums used by battalion parties after ZERO.

(iii) 6 circuits were laid as far as the LANGEMARCK ROAD by 154th Brigade Signal Section on the night of the 18th, but owing to shelling it was found impossible to get lines through to battalions until the night of the 19th. During the battle lines were frequently through for periods of about 20 minutes and important information obtained but despite the use of laddered lines, frequent linemen's posts, and alternate routes continuous telephonic communication could not be ensured.

/Lines,

Lines were through to the left battalion intermittently from 7 a.m. on the 20th to 6.30 p.m. on the 21st., to the right battalions, lines were kept going from dusk on the 19th till shortly after ZERO, but not again working for any appreciable time until dawn on the 21st.

Circuits to Machine Gun Companies detachments via Brigade Advanced Exchange at FERDINAND FARM were maintained throughout successfully.

R.F.A., F.O.O's. The lines laid out by the Artillery across the STEENBEEK – LANGEMARCK ROAD Sector suffered the same fate as the Infantry circuit. 225 Brigade, e.g., never succeeded in getting a line through to RAT HOUSE O.P. and any other circuits laid were cut constantly and soon abandoned. F.O.O.s got through, e.g., from COCKCROFT for a short time but reliance could not be placed on telephone lines and visual was principally used, on occasion F.O.O's used Infantry lines.

All O.P. lines West of the STEENBEEK were successfully maintained and circuits were run to visual stations as at FLEMINGS WOOD communicating with F.O.O.s beyond the barraged area.

(iv) PIGEONS.

Pigeons proved invaluable and were often the only means of communication. Reports were received at Divisional Headquarters from 40 minutes after ZERO until nightfall with great regularity. 64 birds were sent out on the 19th; 20 more at noon on the 20th and 30 at night. On the 20th, 28 messages several duplicated were received. The shortest time messages took from battalion to Brigade was 50 minutes; the longest 3 hours 10 minutes. Most messages took about 1½ hours. The value of pigeons at F.O.O's was again shewn and if possible more will be allotted in future.

(v) BATTALION COMMUNICATIONS.

As arranged the 9th Royal Scots and 4th Seaforths ran forward 2 circuits each immediately after ZERO.

The Seaforths reached PHEASANT FARM at 8.30 a.m. and maintained circuits till 12.30 p.m. 15 messages being sent and received at Battalion Headquarters. After this hour the barrage having shifted no lines stood. No attempt was made to extend lines beyond PHEASANT FARM as the tactical situation did not admit of it.

On the right the signallers of the 9th Royal Scots carried out their programme in a most excellent manner and advancing beyond NEW HOUSES which were found unsuitable for a Signal Station reached FLORA COTTAGE about 6.15 a.m. The Companies of this Battalion were thus in telephonic communication with Battalion Headquarters as soon as they reached their objectives 30 minutes after ZERO. Lines were then continued forward and communication was established with the front Companies of the 7th Argylls by 9.40 a.m. As a result communication by telephone was maintained except for a short period during the afternoon of the 20th, with all the Companies of the two right Battalions. Speech was excellent throughout as far forward as BAVAROISE HOUSE near QUEBEC FARM. These results reflect most creditably upon the

/energy

- 4 -

the energy and determination of the signalling officer of the 7th Argylls and the signalling Sergeant and Signallers of the 9th Royal Scots who carried out the bulk of the work.

(vi) VISUAL.

Visual was successfully used both by Artillery and Infantry from the captured high ground backwards. About 80 messages were sent by the Artillery from BULOW FARM and PHEASANT FARM. Six by the 7th Argylls from QUEBEC FARM and BAVAROISE HOUSE and six by the left battalions from PHEASANT FARM. The 154th Infantry Brigade had a station at CANE POST but beyond picking up forward stations no work was done.

ROCKETS.

The following were fired - out of 24 sent up -

Unit	from	to	time.
4th Gordons	200 yards E. of PHEASANT FARM.	RAT HOUSE	8.00 a.m.
4th Seaforths	1 from DOG HOUSE	FERDINAND FARM	1.00 a.m.
	1 FROM PHEASANT FARM	DOG HOUSE	9.00 a.m.

The 7th Argylls and 9th Royal Scots having telephone communication did not require to use rockets, but the results obtained by the left Division were disappointing.

3. CONCLUSIONS.

The following points were brought out by the experience of the attack:-

(a) Where no buried cables exist no amount of foresight will ensure telephone speech through a barrage. Linemen were posted every 200 yards and shewed the greatest devotion to duty but without much success. There is no shorter road to good communication than a six feet trench.

(b) With foresight battalion communication being for the most part in front of the barraged line, should not present insuperable difficulty. The personnel is excellent and it is in the interests of all concerned to see during this winter that battalion signallers are trained and organised under their own officers. Every assistance in training and providing suitable equipment locally will be given by the Divisional Signal Company.

(c) Power Buzzer and Amplifier proved of some value. It was not rapid but quicker than pigeon. The best message through three transmissions took 40 minutes from Battalion Headquarters to Brigade Headquarters as against the best pigeons 50. The difficulties are at present chiefly technical and better training will obviate them.

(d) The Signal arrangements for the attacking Brigade were arranged and communicated direct to Battalion Signal Officers by the O.C. Divisional Signals. This is obviously a bad principle, but unless Brigade Staffs interest themselves in the practical problems of communications

/it

it is difficult to see what else can be done. The Brigade Signal Officer is not a Staff Officer, and is fully occupied during operations in maintaining touch with his battalions.

(e)   Pigeons were reliable but not rapid. Many birds were lost owing to the men carrying them up going astray. Hardly any birds returned with clips, messages being tied as best they could be. This no doubt accounts for the slow times done in some cases. Battalion pigeon men should be given a definite standing if possible where this has not already been done. The same men should be employed always to fetch birds up, and it is suggested that a distinctive badge be worn by pigeoneers on their signals arm band. This would serve to mark the men definitely.

There is no reason why clips should not be used if it is clearly understood that not to do so will delay birds indefinitely in their flight.

Major R.E.
O.C. 51st Divisional Signal Company

28th September 1917.

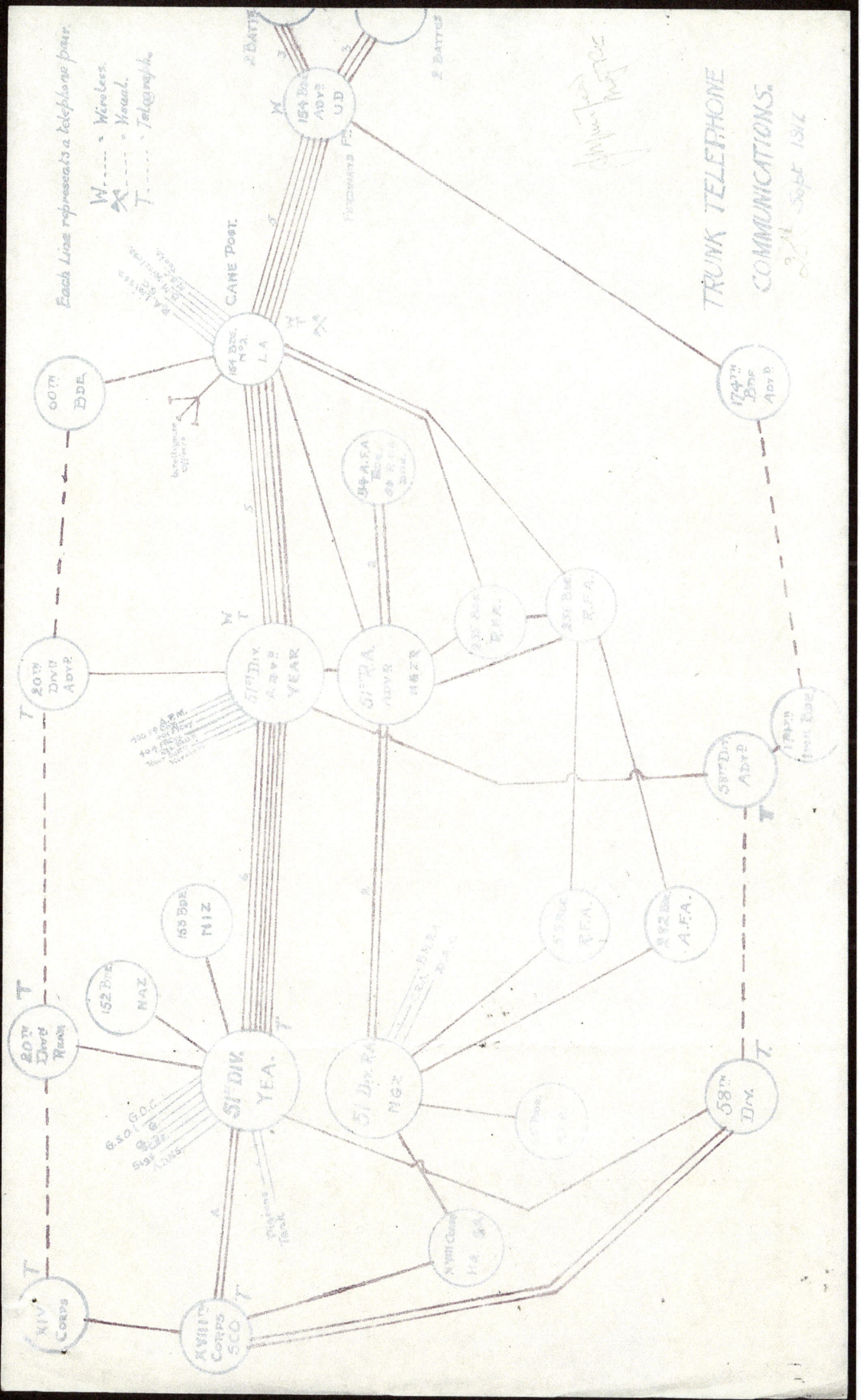

Scheme of Brigade
Communication:

W = Dog   A = Amplifier
W = Pigeon   ⊕ = Power Buzzer
☀ = Visual   W = Wireless Station

Y Day

26th Sept 1917
(Amended)

FIRST OBJECTIVE   SECOND OBJECTIVE

Brigade HQs — Cane Post — Exchange

Brigade Adv. Post — Ferdinand Fm. — Exchange

154 Bde. Signal Section — 3 circuits

Rat House Exchange — Batt HQs

4th Seaforths — 2 circuits — Pheasant Fm. — 4th Gordons — 2 circuits — Bn. Adv. Post

U294 7.6 — Central Amplifier Station

154 Bde. Signal Section — 3 circuits

Bulow Farm Exchange

New Houses — 8th Royal Scots — 2 circuits — 7th Argylls — 2 circuits — Bn. Adv. Post — Coys.

Red House

Bn. HQs.

57 D Signals
Vol 28

CONFIDENTIAL
HIGHLAND DIVISION.

57th (H.) Divnl Signal Co. R.E. (1)

War Diary.

October 1917.

WAR DIARY or INTELLIGENCE SUMMARY.

Army Form C. 2118.

51st (Highland) Signal Coy R.E. T.F.

OCTOBER ~~September~~ 1917   Sheet 1.

Place	Date	Hour	Summary of Events and Information	Remarks and references to Appendices
BONLEUX AU MONT	1/10/17		Checking & checking over stores, equipment, 58th Div. Cd & reconnecting	
	2/10/17		Work on new HQrs.	
	3/4		Work on new HQrs. 153 Bde take over left sect. 50 Div. ft.	
	5/10/17		154 Bde take over left sect. 50 Div. ft. 57 Div HQrs move fr. ACHIET le petit to BOISKEUX au Mont. Echelon B S[pella]ins of 153 & 154 Bde join Div. Sig Cy ft training	
	6/10/17		57 Div. take over command of Corps front section fr. 50 Div. All lines switches over HQrs. No 2 sect. from 6 Army to train. 152 Bde Spell. over 51 Div S. Cy.	
	7/10/17		D°.	
	8/10/17		Work on local circuits & work in Off. Visited all Bdes.	
	9/10/17		4 hr. army't circuit run fr. Div. Train to Argyll in BOISKEUX dn trunk	
	10/10/17		Work on overhead routes & in camp. Visited all Bdes. Buried cables for wire.	
	11/10/17		D°. Inspection of Div. Sigl. School by Lt. Col G.C.	
	12/10/17		D°. 16 pair permalite from QQR to NEUVILLE VITASSE being erected.	
	13/10/17 - 14/10/17		D°. Visited 154 Bde. Hrs. Genl Edwards US Army visited Sigl. Office. Communication explained to him. 50th Div A (250 & 251 Bdes) relieved by 2/3 Div Bde Staff DA & IRA	
	15/10/17		D°. Visited 153 Bde hrs. No 2 Section returns to 152 Bde HQrs. Echelon B S[pella]ins relieved Grant.	
	16/10/17		Maintenance. Rest. circ. completed. 152 Bde relieved 153 Bde	

Army Form C. 2118.

57st (HIGHLAND) SIGNAL COY R.E. T.F.

WAR DIARY or INTELLIGENCE SUMMARY.

OCTOBER 1917   Sheet 2.

(Erase heading not required.)

Instructions regarding War Diaries and Intelligence Summaries are contained in F. S. Regs., Part II. and the Staff Manual respectively. Title pages will be prepared in manuscript.

Place	Date	Hour	Summary of Events and Information	Remarks and references to Appendices
BOISLEUX-AU-MONT	17/10/17		Maintenance & improving circuits. Exchange installed at HENINR for Fwk. Coy R.E. Pioneers & R.E. dump & Livres area.	
	18/19/17		Circuits diverted off old cones to NEUVILLE VITASSE to put them on Pot. R.E. Exchange working.	
	19th–22nd		Work regulating & improving overhead routes. Check of stores & equipment. Wagon Drill. Maj. Gen. Mckay's Staff, U.S.A. Army visit Signal office, & are instructed in methods of communication of Division.	
	23–27th		Regulation of all overhead lines. Rewiring of test pts. 25th 312 Bde RFA (62 Div) relieve 2nd Att. A. Bde 262 Bde RFA go into right R.A. Bde Hqrs. 28th 57th Artillery major Div's went in ACHEUX area. Communication via ACHEUX office.	
	28th		153 Bde moved from BOYELLE to HAUTEVILLE. Communication via XVII Corps (STRUM). 12th Bde relieve 157.	
	29th		154 Bde move to 12EL. Communication via XVII Corps. Work continues on Test pts. circuits.	
	30th		Work on test pts. circuits. Inspection of horses & wagons. Divisional office opens at HERMAVILLE – circuits to XVII Corps 153 & 154 & 3 Bdes.	
	31st		163 Bde relieve 152 Bde, who open at WARLUS. Circuits put thro' to HERMAVILLE. Work on circuits continued.	
	Very quiet month.		Work confined to renewing all overhead routes, which were completed to relieving Division. Forward work confined to maintenance & renewal of faulty circuits. In Western installations all personal lines at VI Corps. Company refitted & brought up to establishment.	Diagram of communications attached.

Montred Major R.E.
O.C. 57th (Highland) Signal Coy R.E. T.F.

51ST HIGHLAND DIVISION
DIAGRAM OF TELEPHONE COMMUNICATION

OCTOBER 1917.

Red = Divisional Circuits
Black = Divisional Artillery Circuits
 = Lines to other Formations
T = Telegraph Office

51st Divisional Engineers

51st DIVISIONAL SIGNAL COMPANY R. E.

NOVEMBER 1917.

Report on Operations attached.

51 D Signal
9/29

Nat(H) Sand signal
R.S.(1)

War Diary.
November 1917.

57th (Highland) Signal Company R.E. T.F.

WAR DIARY or INTELLIGENCE SUMMARY.

Army Form C. 2118.

NOVEMBER 1917

Place	Date	Hour	Summary of Events and Information	Remarks and references to Appendices
BOISLEUX	1/11/17		Reg Dt. left half No 1 Section moves by road to HERMAVILLE. Test point at 99 Completed. Linesmen of 34 Div double ones in wood.	
HERMAVILLE	2/11/17		Div HQ's open HERMAVILLE 10.0 am. Capt Brown & R.A. detail remain at BOISLEUX. HQ's 34 Div. Left half move by road to HERMAVILLE. Staff put in telephone area handed over to 34 Div.	
"	3/11/17		DAPOS & Div Trains on line. PB & amplifier establid at HAPPEQ & HERMAVILLE. Fr. Going to work to Blen in farm village. N Section practice cable laying.	
	4/11/17		Visits IV Corps. 36 Div & reconnoitred area METZ en Couture. Lieut Gould & two lorries with 14 men proceed to METZ Grand Park IV Corps.	
	5/11/17		Visited 36 Div front up to Battalion HQ's. Visited 36 Div & IV Corps. Arrange cable close & work in METZ area	
	6/11/17		Captain Sutherland & 4 NCOs & men proceed to YPRES to work. Note of Communications forwarded to HQ 12 Signal Coy 8th R.S. & 12 & 154 Bde reported fr Wincken Drive	
	7/11/17		Work in METZ area. OC Sigs 152 & 153 Bde visit METZ area. Training of Coy being carried on.	
	8/11/17		Do. Cable demands given to A.D. Sig IV Corps. Conference with Bde S/O about use of future operations.	
	9/11/17		Do. HQ's at YPRES arrd. Visits man n. IV Corps. Note of equipment given to deliver & dugouts Lines asked to be allotted immediately. Visits OC Sigs 152 Bde 152 Bde Sigs Centre asked Centralia	
	10/11/17		Work at HQ's & line in METZ area.	

51st (Highland) Signal Coy R.E.

WAR DIARY
or
INTELLIGENCE SUMMARY.
(Erase heading not required.)

Army Form C. 2118.

NOVEMBER 1917 Sheet 2

Place	Date	Hour	Summary of Events and Information	Remarks and references to Appendices
HERMAVILLE	11/11/17		Visited YPRES Front Tr. Cops & 36 Divn - Bde Hq & 1/4 & 1/7 O/153 recalled	
	12/11/17		Visited YPRES Front Lines - Linesmen all day. Work carried	
	13/11/17		Back to HERMAVILLE entrained for HAMINCOURT wagons & horses for	
	14/11/17		do. Waiting scheme for cable crossings. Work on artillery lines. Visited 153 Coy J G METZ	
	15/11/17		Visited YPRES order. Use lantern for G METZ	
			Relief 152 Use Lantern J. G METZ A	
	16/11/17		E.I.H. Wdy 4/16 CMA Office near Bn HAUTEVILLE	
			Testing lines down to HAUTEVILLE & Transport back 2 J G	
			MOYENNEVILLE with Maj Pack & B	
	17/11/17		Fullk lorries G YPRES 2nd in Comd staff on Italy. Halts at Ablery	
LITTLE			Frd G Pack (on) Cackle & Jernives & Linesmen 2 & b-G. To the Brigade	
1st Cav			Lines from Tr. Cops to Bn Transport lines G YPRES 153 Coy G.H. night	
HQ 15th			S.J. ROSENICOURT 153 at BAPAUME. Communications had Bn.C.G.P. now	
	18/11/17		Testing out forward lines, 2 running alarms	
	19/11/17		All circuits put through successfully. 152 & 153 BE is lined TRESCAULT, 158 at METZ	
			ADS 400 FA Cy Pioneers. Transport of all cages 4 & 5" HA Bde 7" 30b, 253, 175 HPA	
			Bde 23 Pagn Left III Cp Waldron 62 DW, 62 DA 86 2 DW	
			Rear Brewy Stn HAYRINCOURT but J. Wire Cav. Engine steam in HAYRINCOURT wood

51st Sgnl Co RE TF.   NOVEMBER 1917.   Sheet 3

Army Form C. 2118.

WAR DIARY or INTELLIGENCE SUMMARY.
(Erase heading not required.)

Place	Date	Hour	Summary of Events and Information	Remarks and references to Appendices
YPRES	19/11/17	7.6p	All cable circuits found as arranged	
		8.30p	All wireless stations in waiting - nothing. 8.30pm - OK. relieved by 153rd Bde.	
	20/11/17	5.30am	All lines OK except line to Maori Bazaar Station - OK 6.45am.	
		6.20am	51st Div/152 & 153 Bde) attack, headed by D & E Battalion Tanks. 7.0am. No 1 Section 2 P Cable Section moves METZ where they park.	
		7.30am	Forward parties started in both Brigade fronts. Through in place to Battle support line at 8.45am. 7.30am 20 pigeons delivered to 153rd Bde.	
		8.45am	2nd Amplifier sent forward. Message received at Q by Board "Triangle Support Captured". 2nd Wireless Stations move up to CLAY STREET.	
		8.45a	Loop through from K.35 a 9.9 (2nd Forward Station 153 Bde). 9.0am 153 Bde Fwd Station through in phase Sgt Burrows & (Pigeonner went at 8.45)	
		9.35a	Q manual station working well, many messages received. 10.0am Left Bde Fwd station in phase of German front line	
		10.10a	1st Pigeon message from No 1 Platoon 6 Black Watch Purple Alteration released 9.15am.	
		10.30a	P Cable section 2 Rpt Left No 1 Section orders up to 153 Bde HQrs to Front.	
		11.15a	Left half mixed up cable sent up in lorry. Capt Sutherland goes up to 163 HQS. List here En. reports symptom of Cavalry	
			passed BIRKEL 11.15am. Visual not possible to FLESQUIERES owing to mist - thro' known to lines Pt BECOURT - MAR PINCON Q C	
		12.5pm	P Cable Section orders to put up poles from Q 5 C 9.6.15 to Q 5 central to then forward to K 36 a 0.3. Rpt they No 1	
			section to ple 132 Bde cable on Coy 2 E's up todo.	
		12.25.	Lieut Cutts reports power through established in communication at K.36 a 2.2 and K.35 a 9.9. No message	
			to and Group to find central amplifier. Visual works from Q to Railway Wireless station (2 orders) orders to Pt BECOURT.	

51st S.Tel Company R.E. T.F.   NOVEMBER 1917. Sheet 4.

Army Form C. 2118.

WAR DIARY
or
INTELLIGENCE SUMMARY.
(Erase heading not required.)

Instructions regarding War Diaries and Intelligence Summaries are contained in F. S. Regs., Part II. and the Staff Manual respectively. Title pages will be prepared in manuscript.

Place	Date	Hour	Summary of Events and Information	Remarks and references to Appendices
YTRES.	26/11/17	1.15p	Cable Section arrived at TRESCAULT & gave forward Instruction given to Captain Sutherland that it astroli appears very erro in forward valley. Tones & wagons are not to be posted on it also & pole transport & lines laid by horses.	
		1.27p	Sig 153 Bde reports 2 D3 pairs as far as K35a 95.85 laid & thro.	
		2.4p	Left Half details 800 to S of 152 Bde HQ — Complete section has joined up. CSM instructed to return to D.HQ	
		3.0p	FF Wireless Station established [crossed out] at Church at RIBECOURT. Station unable to get in touch with	
			OC. 1/6 Gordon Highlanders and say he is in touch with 152 Bde by Wireless.	
		5.0pm	Captn Sutherland returns from RIBECOURT. Reports 2 pr funkets D3 laid on poles as far as K36a0.5. and 2	
			pair D laid on left of road & parallel to other lines. Cable Section, No 1 Section turnover for the night	
			at the NE of Hermies cut Wood.	
		7.45p	Instructions sent to No 1 Section & Postc to continue above & outlet say to & run out armoured quad	
			from D5 K26 a 2.2.	
		10.30p	Instructions that 152 & 153 Bde will probably move at dawn to K36 B 2.2.2 & K32 d g. Lent guard ordered to form YBrH Hqrs at 153 Bde HQs in morning. FF Wireless station orders to move to	
			K 32c 5.3 & report hearings 5th Seaforths at daybreak.	

Army Form C. 2118.

WAR DIARY
or
INTELLIGENCE SUMMARY.
(Erase heading not required.)

Sheet No 5

Instructions regarding War Diaries and Intelligence Summaries are contained in F. S. Regs., Part II. and the Staff Manual respectively. Title pages will be prepared in manuscript.

Place	Date	Hour	Summary of Events and Information	Remarks and references to Appendices
YPRES.			Reconnaissance finds:	
21/11/17	7a	Lieut Jarrott & Rly — Lieut McDermid & Cables sects. both div'n line running up to Cdn Rly corner road.	
TRESCAULT		10.30	Div HQrs here to TRESCAULT — 152 Bde & 153 Bde in German support line. 154 Bde in old Brit. Bde 152 Bde.	
		10.30	Rly Rly proceed continue 2 points to RIBECOURT. P.Sects lay a latral to 153 Bde R 152 HQs.	
			152 Bde move to Hermes 153 HQs.	
		1.40	62 Bde to Flesquieres. Int of Cach — 200 cables actin' pushed up.	
		2.30p	2/Lg aerie RIBECOURT — lay 2 field pairs to FLESQUIERES. 3 of FF Winches tabby with S/waffle.	
				Int Bde Mc corris
		5.0p	Thof to FLESQUIERES. Thof to 2Bde Bd of RIBECOURT.	
		9.0p	T/p to Bde RFA RIBECOURT. 2/Lg orders 2/p the line RIBECOURT to FLESQUIERES R/Lelly ordered to lay RIBECOURT to TRESCAULT. After settled & 7p to Havrincourt tomorrow. FF stat ordered to CANTAING. RA Sect. established at FLESQUIERES, also RA Bde line in.	
TRESCAULT	22/11/17	10am	Div HQrs move to FLESQUIERES.Move 152 Bde & Div line HQ. LA JUSTICE FARM. 2 half div HQ G	
		7am	lay 2 pair field cable to FLESQUIERES. Reconnoitred Bde lines laid. FLESQUIERES. Left O RTR	
			Rell complete work overseeing. FF stat at CANTAING, FC at FLESQUIERES.	
	23/11/17	1.0am	Div HQrs move to Flesquieres at 10am, 152 Bde take over line with HQrs at LA JUSTICE FARM. LA JUSTICE FARM	
			G half No 1 Sect. install. to lay 2 pair field cable FLESQUIERES to LA JUSTICE FARM	

Army Form C. 2118.

WAR DIARY
or
INTELLIGENCE SUMMARY.
(Erase heading not required.)

Sheet 6

Instructions regarding War Diaries and Intelligence Summaries are contained in F. S. Regs., Part II. and the Staff Manual respectively. Title pages will be prepared in manuscript.

Place	Date	Hour	Summary of Events and Information	Remarks and references to Appendices
TRESCAULT	23/4/17	1 a.m.	B Sec RE left orders to lay one line from LA JUSTICE FARM to HAVRINCOURT & connect 152 & 119 Bde (40 Div). Cable were in a completion to back up of ORIVAL WOOD. A Set G refer to it to FLESQUIERES.	
		6 a.m.	R. & 2 speakers lines via FLESQUIERES. Interrupted by wireless personnel of Div HQ in garden by German P.E. Dump. One pair run to R.A. Exchange, one pair to G.T.54 Bde Exchange, P cable section runs 7 pr cable in extension to work on B.Lt.	
		7.58 a.m.	All lines seem no issues alive. Direct telephone had a 2 pm to LA JUSTICE, met RA Liaison 1 p. G. to 152 Bde. "A" Sec. runs a new pair to 253 Bde RFA between FLESQUIERES & HAVRINCOURT. Extension at ORIVAL WOOD Bde & Sig. Office & TRESCAULT.	
		10 a.m.	D.HQ opened. R.S Sigl. work from Cliffords to Sigl off. & D.S Sigl Office Telegrams 1 to G.T.54 Bde office.	
		12.37	Cable arrives for run. One section flood up, 2 mile D.3 issued to each Rgt & Bde	
		3 p.m.	Line to TRESCAULT down	
		6.31	TRESCAULT line through - due to large bodys of CAVALRY all over the country D.H.Q exchange busy all day. One line first of FLESQUIERES successfully maintained though so close to 5 minutes. This the first time field cable run since 1914.	

(A7585) Wt. W807/M1672 350,000 4/17 Sch. 52a. Forms/C/2118/14

WAR DIARY
or
INTELLIGENCE SUMMARY.

Army Form C. 2118.

Sheet No 7

Place	Date	Hour	Summary of Events and Information	Remarks and references to Appendices
FLESQUIERES	23/4/17	7pm	Orders to hand over to Guards Divl. Wired for an officer to return to refit Flesquieres as soon as possible. FF W/T station attacked by a shell, one will drawn.	
	24/4/17	7.6 am	No 1 Section moves GYTRE to LITTLEWOOD, rendezvous 12 noon. Handed over to Guards. RA Section moves LITTLESQUIERES to take new advance party on boy to THENENCOURT & then to BAIZIEUX - Communicate established 12 noon. Windless section moved to TRESCAULT, also with No 1 section.	
		12.0 no	No 1 Section rendezvous moved to BEAULENCOURT.	
		4.0 pm	4 lorries stolen from an Army S.C. & slots there sent for YTRE to BAIZIEUX 2 lorries move store & personnel of TRESCAULT to BAIZIEUX W/T section by team to BAIZIEUX. E.O. pm. To station appended at ALBERT & sent to BAIZIEUX Telephone lost run & staff a telephone service to telephone to 55 Coy.	
BAIZIEUX	25/4/17	2.0 am	Long party arrive.	
		5.0 am	Wireless section arrives.	
		1.0 pm	Settle into BAIZIEUX Chateau.	
			No 1 Section arrives Quard.	
	26th-28th		Refitting at BAIZIEUX.	
	30th	2.0 pm	Orders received to return to battle area. 4.0 pm. Advance party & Louis sent to LECHELLE to join 57 Divl Office. Company held in readiness to move.	

OM Pritchard Major RE
OC 1 Sig Co 57 Divl

G.
    51st (H) Division   FE/312

        Herewith report on Communications during the recent operations.

                                                    Major R.E.
5/12/17   O.C. 51st (H) Divnl Signal Co R.E. (T)

51st (H) Divisional Signal Co R.E. (T)

Report on Communications between TRESCAULT and FONTAINE during operations of 20th - 24th November 1917.

Ref. Maps 57c N.E. 1/10,000
57c S.E. 1/10,000

1. Preparation.

The Signal communications for these operations had to be evolved in a fortnight out of what existed to supply one Artillery and one Infantry Brigade only. Fortunately, a good bury had already been completed from the South edge of HAVRINCOURT WOOD to BILHEM FARM in the support line, and by using this as the backbone of the system and by running short spurs and one or two alternative routes on poles or in communication trenches, all necessary communications were provided by ZERO. About a dozen test points had in addition to be completed or re-wired, as and as fighting troops only reached the sector at the most 36 hours before the battle and no telephones were permitted before Zero a good deal of arrangement was required both to lay a sufficient system and to hand it over fool-proof to formations as they came into position. This was successfully accomplished in every particular.

The telephone system was exactly similar to that used in previous attacks and was as exemplified in the attached theoretical diagram. No difficulty whatever was experienced during the battle with these prepared communications and no alterations in the system are proposed for future operations.

11. During Operations.

Novr. 20th 1917.

The buried cable system ended in a dugout in DERBY RESERVE trench. Before Zero lines were laid from this point to a central sap-head on each Brigade front from which forward parties started. Additional circuits were allotted before Zero on the buried cable route for the use of each Infantry and Artillery Brigade, so that forward parties were enabled to keep in touch with Brigade Headquarters without interfering with circuits in use at zero hour

During the advance of the 152 and 153 Brigades communication was uninteruptedly maintained by telephone to Battalions and generally to Companies. Battalion Signallers first laid out one earth return circuit per Battalion, looping these lines into previously selected German dugouts in the various enemy lines passed. These Battalion parties were followed immediately by Brigade parties laying out two twisted telephone pairs to the same points. Telephonic communication with Unseen support trenc was established about 80 minutes after Zero and communication by lamp was obtained about the same time from the slope beyond The GRANDE RAVINE

Artillery parties laid out one pair per Artillery Brigade at the same time as the Infantry Brigade parties; in some cases
.adding/

adding a second circuit later. On the move forward of Batteries these lines served to connect Artillery Brigades with their batteries, and the forward portions were used by F.O.Os.

The Divisional Cable Wagons reached METZ before 8 a.m. on the 20th and by noon four Divisional Cable detachments and "P" Cable Section (Attached from lV Corps) were proceeding over the old front line. By 4.0 p.m. on the 20th four twisted Cable pairs on poles had been laid as far as K 36 a 0.5 by these sections. The personnel of these sections had been distributed before Zero in test points from METZ to BILHEM and it was successfully collected, mounted and working in cable laying parties by noon.

During the operations from the 20th to the 24th visual by Lucas Lamp was in full use between Companies, Battalions and Infantry Brigades and between F.O.Os, Field Batteries and Artillery Brigades. A Divisional visual station at BILHEM FARM received messages from 8.30 a.m. on 20th. when the capture of TRIANGLE SUPPORT was notified, up to midnight on the 20th. Messages were received by this station from all over the forward slope as far as FLESQUIRIES.

Power Buzzers and Amplifiers moved forward as arranged One power Buzzer each moved forward with Brigade forward parties, one power buzzer with each of the two Battalions of the second wave of each Brigade. One combined Amplifier and Power Buzzer station was established before zero in a dugout in CLAY STREET and was in touch two hours after zero with the Power Buzzers at Brigade Forward stations. A second combined Amplifier and Power Buzzer moved forward to UNSEEN TRENCH three hours after zero and was in touch almost immediately after with the Power Buzzers with Battalions on the FLESQUIRIES RIDGE. Telephone lines holding for the most part, only a few messages were sent by these earth induction sets but all those sent were received by the Amplifiers and duly forwarded.

One Wireless Station was established before Zero at 152 Brigade Hqrs. at TRESCAULT and was in touch at zero with the Corps directing stations. At 12.30p.m. a second station, up to then held in reserve in a dugout in the front line, was ordered forward, taking with it in addition to the squad already detailed for it, the personnel of the rear amplifier station. At 3 p.m. this station was in communication from RIBECOURT CHURCH with 152 Brigade Hqrs. at TRESCAULT. A few messages were sent and received during the afternoon.

November 21st 1917.

During the second day of the battle more difficulty was experienced owing to the frequent moves of Hqrs. no timely notification of which reached the Signal Service in several occasions. Divisional Hqrs. were moved to TRESCAULT at 10.30 a.m. and put on arrival in touch by telephone with all Brigades and the Corps. The Divisional advanced Exchange at HAVRINCOURT WOOD was closed, but the Artillery exchange at the same place was not moved forward to TRESCAULT until the afternoon circuits for the use of the C.R.A. being put through backwards from TRESCAULT to the wood and Artillery Brigades still being connected with the exchange in the wood Communication to the 152 Brigade at RIBECOURT was effected by means of the poled lines laid on the 20th and to the 153 Brigade at K 29 d 2.5 by means of the two pairs laid by the Brigade forward party. A lateral line connecting with the poled/

poled route was also laid from K 36 a 2.5. to 153 Brigade Hqrs.

154 Brigade moved on the morning of the 21st to a dugout in front of TRESCAULT and was in touch by telephone to Divisional Headquarters up to about 11 a.m. After this time however telephonic communication to the Brigade was lost, The Brigade moving forward without notice and its destination being unknown. Two twisted pairs of cable were laid and poled by the Divnl. Sections from Ribecourt to FLESQUIRIES where it was discovered 154 Bde. had established its Hqrs. and by 5 p.m. telephonic communication was reestablished.

Artillery Brigades had moved forward by nightfall to RIBECOURT and FLESQUIRIES. Telephonic communication was maintained to these Brigades during the day by means of the lines laid forward on the 20th by Artillery Parties. In the afternoon and artillery exchange was established at FLESQUIRIES to which the Artillery Brigades laid lines and were thus in touch with the Artillery Liason Officer at 154 Brigade Hqrs. The 154 Bde on arrival at Flesquiries laid out lines to its Battalions and established by the afternoon telephonic communication as far forward as FONTAINE.

Considerable use was made by 153 Brigade on the 21st of German overhead lines East of FLESQUIRIES.

During the 21st as previously arranged Power Buzzers and Amplifiers were discarded and the Wireless personnel concentrated into two Wireless squads. Surplus Infantry personnel were withdrawn with their stores to TRESCAULT. The Wireless Station at TRESCAULT moved on the afternoon of the 21st to FLESQUIRIES and that at RIBECOURT opened just West of MARCOING (5th Seaforth Hqrs) at 3 p.m. This station was subsequently moved to CANTAING from which place communication was opened at 7 a.m. on the 22nd.

November 22nd. 1917.

During this day work was confined to improvements to existing lines and maintenance. Telephone speech was possible throughout the whole Division practically all day. Reconnaissances were made of the German communications throughout the area but it was found that little use could be made of these in the limited time available.

November 23rd. 1917.

On the 23rd Divnl Hqrs moved to FLESQUIRIES at 10 a.m. and 152 Bde. Hqrs moved to La JUSTICE FARM. The position of other formations remained as on 22nd. Communications for this situation were laid entirely between dawn and 10 a.m. by the Signal Company. The Divisional Cable Sections laid field Cable pairs from their cable wagons from FLESQUIRIES to 152 Bde. Hqrs, from 152 Bde. Hqrs to the 119th Bde in GRAINCOURT and to Artillery Brigade Hqrs from the Artillery Exchange in FLESQUIRIES. 152 Bdigade Signal Section ran out lines to all Battalions of the Brigade at the same time.

The Divisional communications on this day approached a system which would obtain in moving warfare. Lines laid forward were not brought on to a telephone exchange but direct telephones were provided between Divisional and Brigade Staffs The exchanges existing at FLESQUIRIES viz; 154 Bde. exchange and the Artillery Liason exchange were utilised to provide communications with rear Hqrs at TRESCAULT the two Brigades in support and the Artillery Brigades. The C.R.A. was given a direct line to his Liason Officer at 152 Brigade. No Signal Staff was utilised for communications forward of FLESQUIRIES

all/

all reports being received direct by the staff on the telephone. This was a great saving in personnel. A Divisional Signal Officer stood by in charge of the circuits at Divisional and Brigade Hqrs. Communications were successfully maintained to all units during this day by mounted linemen although frequently cut by shelling and by tanks. There was a good deal of trouble however owing to large bodies of cavalry and tanks in the area behind FLESQUIRIES.

111. These operations presented the Signal Service with a novel and difficult situation. There was continual movement of Hqrs; the roads and tracks were blocked with transport and although lines were seldom cut by shellfire, tanks and large bodies of cavalry and artillery played havoc with telephone wires even when poled. Maintenance and the movement of Signal personnel were accordingly rendered very difficult and the strain of continous work day and night proved severe. It did not appear also to be sufficiently realised in all cases that the decisive factor in the movement and position of Hqrs. ought to be communications. The failure on the 21st to keep really adequate communications between Division and Brigades was due largely to lack of co-operation in this matter. For example information was received on the afternoon of the 20th that 152 Bde. would move to RIBECOURT - off the line previously determined for communications. A Wireless station was at once sent there in preparation and other arrangements made. This move was subsequently cancelled and the new Hqrs fixed at K 36 a 2.5 Lines were hastily laid there and parties, engaged according to programme in building a poled route across country to FLESQUIRIES, diverted to assist. A Signal Office and exchange were established at K 36 a 2.5 when the Brigade again decided to move to RIBECOURT and work had to be recommenced. Such moves can be coped with when really mobile conditions are reached - e.g. the move to FLESQUIRIES and LA JUSTICE FARM But before open country is reached and transport can move freely there is an intermediate stage of congestion when it is imperative that moves of Hqrs. should be determined carefully and full warning given. It is suggested that since telephones are a sine qua non the technical difficulties in providing telephones in moving warfare and are much greater than those met with in working with by vibrator, in future operations which develop into semi-open fighting no attempt should be made to keep touch with units by several separate systems. One main route of three or four poled cables would be run to a succession of previously selected points in the centre of the Divisional Sector and small exchanges established at these points. As soon as an exchange was ready in the forward area Hqrs of Infantry and Artillery Brigades would be informed and would move to the vicinity of these exchanges. In the recent fighting this would have worked as follows. Forward Signal parties would have laid their lines as previously decided upon up to and beyond FLESQUIRIES RIDGE. Divisional parties would have run a poled route across country to the village and established a small exchange there. As soon as this exchange was running forward parties would have looped their forward lines into it and Bde. Hqrs. would then have moved to within a short distance of the exchange. The Divisional parties would have laid spurs to connect these Hqrs to the exchange and would have continued poling a route as far forward as possible in the direction of CANTAING preparatory to a further move.

It is in short suggested that moves of Hqrs should as far as possible be regulated by the progress of telephone routes up/

up to the point when the cable wagons can be used in open country.   A diagram of these proposals is attached.

lV Auxiliary means of Communication.

(a) Rockets.

None of these were used.

(b) Runners.

The going being good and there being little shelling runners proved invaluable.   Mounted orderlies were provided by King Edwars's Horse for the Brigades and the Division. and were very useful.   Motor Cycles could not be used and the Signal Dispatch Riders were also mounted.

(c) Pigeons.

These proved a great disappointment.   Two messages only were received on the 20th, seven on the 21st (5 of which were practice messages) and eight on the 22nd. (4 of which were practice messages).   It was not indeed necessary to depend on pigeons but this experience shows that in misty weather very poor results are obtained by carrier pigeons.

(d) Visual.

Visual Signalling both by shutter and lamp was used throughout with great success.   The standard of signalling proved excellent.

(e) Wireless.

The experiment was made of having all Wireless and earth induction personnel under Divnl Control.   24 Signallers from the Infantry and Pioneers were previously attached to the Divisional Signal Company and placed under the Command of Lieut Coutts, 4th Seaforths, also attached to the Company.
The scheme for the employment of wireless in these operations was carried out in practice for ten days at HERM- AVILLE and every man knew his task.   The result was a far better use of Wireless than ever obtained before.   All Power Buzzers and Amplifiers reached there positions and communication was obtained exactly as desired.   The transition from Earth Induction sets to ardinary Wireless working was successfully made and very good results were obtained by trench Wireless stations.   Over 80 messages were sent and received during three days working.   The stations were pushed well forward e.g. the RIBECOURT station was in the village before the enemy was out of FLESQUIERES and was sniped from the High ground all afternoon.
It is proposed to alter slightly the future organisation of Wireless in the Division as it is considered that the experience of YPRES and CAMBRAI shows that the single working power buzzer station is only of use in exceptional circumstances.   These instruments will be retained at Divnl. Hqrs. and issued if required, instruments being given to a proportion/

proportion of Battalion Signallers in their use. An additional Wireless Station will be organised together with two Power Buzzer and Amplifier Stations and for this purpose 14 Signallers instead of 24 will be required, as detailed in a separate memo previously forwarded.

V. The supply of cable was not sufficient to meet any but the most essential demands and it is important that all units should realise that had our advance continued another day there would have been practically no field cable in the Corps. Economy in in the use of cable can however only be ensured by avoiding unnecessary movement of Hqrs. During operations cable dumps were formed first at the front line, secondly at the crater and finally at FLESQUIRES and sufficient cable was conveyed by the Signal Company forward to meet urgent requirements.

VI Personnel

As mobile conditions were anticipated it was not considered advisable to attempt any pooling of Signal Personnel and all units worked successfully with their own establishment.

Major R.E.

30/11/17   O.C. 51st (H) Divnl Signal Co R.E. (T)

51st (Highland) Divisional Signal Coy. R.E. T.F.
Theoretical Diagram of Communication prior to an attack.   30/4/17.

Lateral Communication not shewn.
Artillery Brigades which are not
Groups have no direct circuit
to Infantry Brigades, but
have a direct circuit to
their ... up in addition to
one to the R.A Exchange.

Nodes and connections:

- **Cable Head** — connected to Front Line, O.P., Amplifier Station, Starting Point for Forward Parties, Batty H.Q.
- **Infantry Brigade** — Divisional Wireless Station, M.G. Coy, Divisional Visual Station
- **Artillery Group** — Batteries
- **Div. Advanced Exchange** — Advanced Dressing Station, Divisional O.P., Field Coy, Pioneers, Road Store, Brigade Transport
- **Div. R.A. Adv. Exchange**
- **Div Exchange** — Corps Wireless Station, Pigeon Loft
- **R.A. Exchange** — D.A.C.

British Front Line

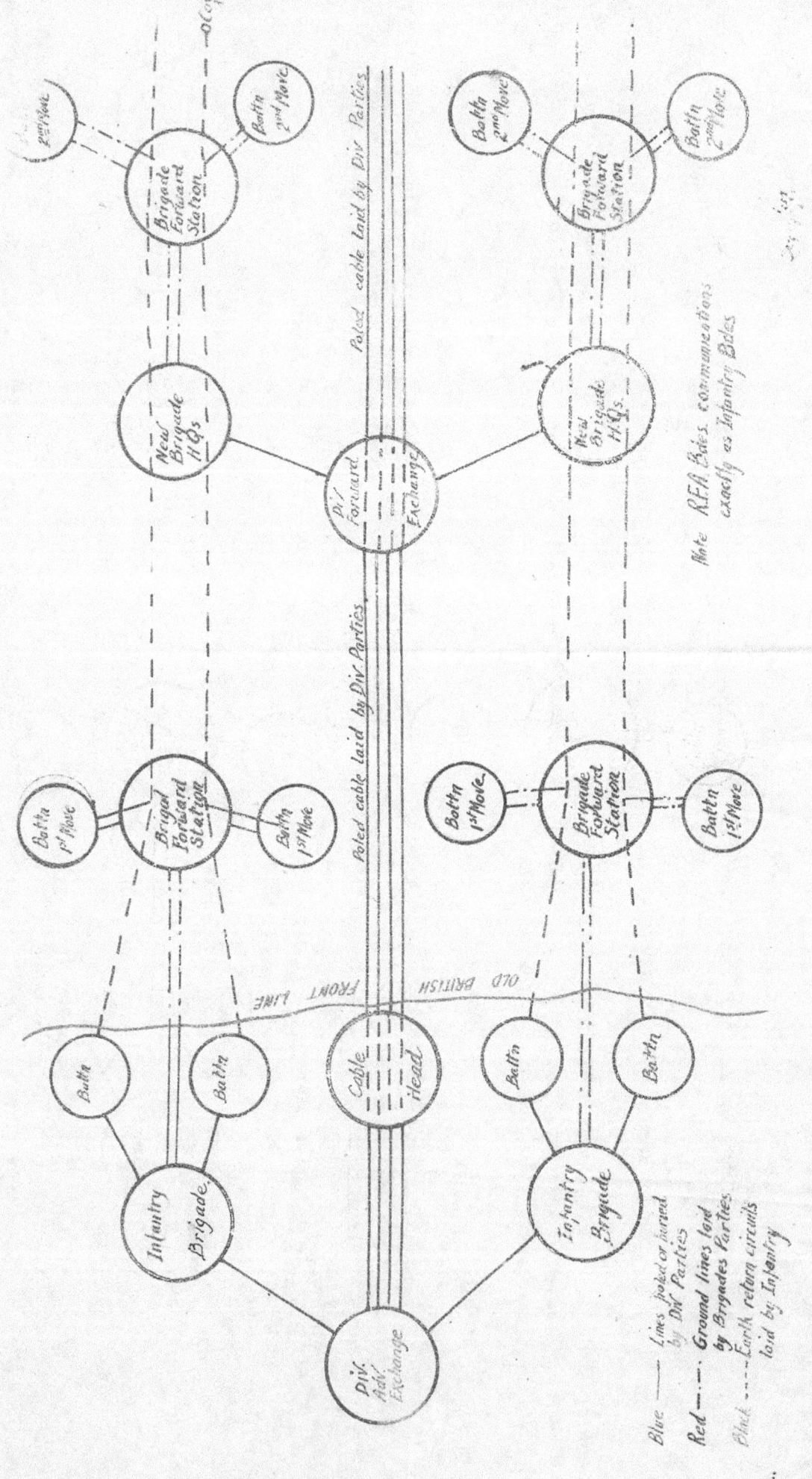

51 D Signals
VA 30

War Diary
for
December 1917

51st(H.) Divl Sig. Co. O.B. (L.)

51st Signal Company R.E. T.F.   SHEET 1.

WAR DIARY or INTELLIGENCE SUMMARY

DECEMBER 1917   Army Form C. 2118

Place	Date	Hour	Summary of Events and Information	Remarks and references to Appendices
LECHELLE	1/12/17	12:N	O/C DHQ obsn at LECHELLE. Cancel R.I. to Staff IV Corps	
		4h		
YPRES		9 am	YPRES. Circuit K offs & W. Cops. B/Talk on IV Corps	
			Wires received extrct via 5½ Div funls, 153 & 154 Bdes wires to 5½ Div wires	
			Visits 5½ Div & arrangemts made.	
	2/12/17	7.0A	Transport arrived with remount dog having marched from BAIZIEUX	
			C/Hors S.M.s W./Cpls Pees & Drivers got 5½ D's arms & tin res. Horses sent	
			over to 5½ D's H.Q. 5½ Sigs & instrumts released	
FREMICOURT	3/12/17	10.0am	Div. HQrs. move to FREMICOURT. 153 & 154 Bdes in line. All roads gave over & necessary alterations	
			Staff put on telephone also Bdes, & Div train. Wireless station installed E. of DOIGNIES. Visual reconnoitred.	
	4/12/17		All communication gone over. Visits Bdes in line. Lovers van Exchange close & kept thro. Arrangement	
			made for retirement to old Bristol line & for conversion of exists circuits to suit e.g. Bgde front. BEAUMETZ	
			have Div. for Exchange & circuits put that direct to D.H. Infantry & 280 F.A. Bdes. Wireless station installed	
			at 153 Bde HQrs. Electric Light & DHQ improved	
	5/12/17		152 Bde take over Div front on retirement to old Bristol front line. All Bdes through in phone. Various circuits	
			altered to suit to Bde night put through. 3 farms from VI Corps put on exchange. 153 Bde at BANKVILLE on	
			3rd Div Exchange 154 Bde at FREMICOURT exchange. Re-bunches of Bde lines at BEUGNY to reduce	

WAR DIARY or INTELLIGENCE SUMMARY

Army Form C. 2118

57th Signal Company 10E.T.F.

Sheet 2.

DECEMBER 1917

Place	Date	Hour	Summary of Events and Information	Remarks and references to Appendices
FREMICOURT	6/12/17		Maintenance. Liaison lines. Arty J. Bn to Bns put through. Some shelling & heavy round Div H.Qs, no damage to overhead wires. I.C. Cpl Th S.S. put in for rec. Repeated communication in late battle sent to Staff.	
	7/12/17		Wires on 152 Bde same. 152 Bde Transport Pal. a telephone. Wireless station installed at 152 D.K Art Station (NE corner of LOUVERVAL Wood) — stations now working — Adv Bde (JM) Bde (JM) Div (FoJ) — all in touch with Coln D.S. at HERMIES.	
	8/12/17		2/c EASTON 3/c CAMPBELL & 2/Lieut HUNT awarded Military Medal by 2/Lieuts J & 2 Bdes NoV. Maintenance. Visited O.D.D. signals Third Army. Office being moved.	
	9/12/17		2 circuits put through to 25th Divn in FREMICOURT (& MARCHES) & Bde ggrvits LAGNICOURT ECOUST. Put ut filts of ut 152 Bde HQs in Ecoust and at I 12 6.5.3	
	10/& 11th		Maintenance 133 Bde relieve 152 Bde 1/4x & 10/11. Circuit Bz Early Exchange put through. Burying of office continued. Camp sandbags & other rose putades against bombs. 51 DivArty (255 & 253 Bgds RFA) relieve 59th Div Arty (295 & 296 Bdes RFA). Capt Brown Arty Sign officer went to Brown 10th Capt Ruddle attaching.	
	12 + 13		Maintenance. 173 Bde RFA and 7th RHA relieved by 5th ARFA & 310 RFA. 0/C work through H.Q.	
	14/14th		Mr Kemp + party laid dir Lpenty arm wire farty D lines from BZ exchange to Leyth Arty Group on means of comm by difficult wet from railway lines. Lt (oct Capt) J Bruce awarded Military Cross today. Ordinary maintenance & improvement of T — BZ route particular.	

31st Signal Co R.E. T.F. — Sheet 3

WAR DIARY or INTELLIGENCE SUMMARY

Army Form C. 2118.

DECEMBER 1917

Place	Date	Hour	Summary of Events and Information	Remarks and references to Appendices
Jerusalem	15/12/17		Lt Smith returned from leave today and took on duties of Arty Sigs. Officer.	
			Arrangements of wires, wireless, telephones signal M'ce between It. Coals. Divisions underway.	
	16/12/17		Signal M'ces improvements proceed. Arty Sig's M'ces very improved.	
	17/12/17		152nd relieved 153 in line. FT D.10 roads thoroughly overhauled at pushing sig arty.	
	18/12/17		Considerable work in staying wires over to arm stores.	
	19/12/17		Buses to drive front parties out of J.M. I found roads had to be abandoned as the	
			lines being front. Still cannot locate all permanent roads.	
	22/23		During the night the 153 Bde relieved the 15th and the 162 Bde in the right	
			section of our front. No casualties. All Bde. at B'quarters. The 2nd Bde made	
			casualties at GHQ & All Bde. at b.H.Q at 9 P.M. 23rd All changes there was	
			complete all that hour. A/C. made a 3.3 TL & German aeroplane bombed Jerus	
			Hope & others are in camp on night hours. The F.F.F.A. gate and F.F.M.O.nts	
			were taken by Unknown section. Brought to H.Q to all and by the reserve the	
			returned about 9 P.M. As a casualty in signals authentic patches postulate the	
			rest of the Signal M'ces.	
	24/12/17		Busily engaged laying Code first cables to protruch maintenance founder-	

WAR DIARY or INTELLIGENCE SUMMARY

Army Form C. 2118.

51st Signal Coy R.E. T.F.   Sheet 4

December 1917

Place	Date	Hour	Summary of Events and Information	Remarks and references to Appendices
Fremicourt	25/12/17		Maintenance of routes. Bank party & battery being provided with —	
	26&27/12/17		Increased power allotted towards the right. 152 Bde taking over part of 2nd Bde front as far as E6A6½d while 153 Bde take over part of 152nd anfers at D29.A.7.3 and 25th Divn (74 Bde) take over part 153 Bde as at D21.d.9.4. Changes completed by 10 AM on 27th inst. Lt Smith 153 Bde went on leave on 27th and 2/Lt Bonneville took over his Bde duties.	
	28/12/17		Test messages and no new work. Traffic. Staff maintenance as 13th Signalling run.	
	29/12/17		new lines to new Bde HQ.	
	30/12/17		154th Bde relieved 152nd on night of 30/31.	
	31/12/17		no new work carried out. DJ	
			Maintenance of lines as usual.	

J M MacRae
Major
OC 51st (Highland) Divnl Sigl
Coy R.E.

Vol 31

51st (H.) Divnl Signal Co. 1

War Diary
of
January 1918.

575 (H Army) Divisional
Signal Coy R.E.
JANUARY 1918
Sheet I

Army Form C. 2118.

WAR DIARY
or
INTELLIGENCE SUMMARY.
(Erase heading not required.)

Instructions regarding War Diaries and Intelligence Summaries are contained in F. S. Regs., Part II. and the Staff Manual respectively. Title pages will be prepared in manuscript.

Place	Date	Hour	Summary of Events and Information	Remarks and references to Appendices
FREMICOURT	1/1/18		Maintenance	
	2/1/18		Maintenance. OC Signals returns from leave.	
	3/1/18		Maintenance. Signal School (1/25 OR ranks) assembles at DHQ & is housed in hutments. Middlesex camp. Parts of buried cables re-sited BEAUMETZ to	
DEMICOURT				
	4/1/18		Parts of bury from left Bde to LOUVERVAL recentrusted. Sgt Steen awarded M.S.M.	
	5/1/18		Maintenance. Wireless station moves from LOUVERVAL (6 sectors) and F.H. DOIGNIES (centre Batt sgt Bde)	
	6/1/18		Maintenance. 152 Bde Cubicle 157 in night sector.	
	7/1/18		Maintenance.	
	8/1/18		Burying cable commenced on line BEAUMETZ – DOIGNIES. 350 men of q men, 50 st 4 pm to 7.00 at 4 pm 1 day party working from BEAUMETZ. N.R.H. party from DOIGNIES – 49 bam bury laid. 600 yds bury Beaumetz end completed. 300 yds bury a caved in DOIGNIES end	
	10/1/18		Work on bury continued. 800 yards completed BEAUMETZ end, 400 of which extends in -250 yards portion of bury within DOIGNIES end – party shelled off job with some casualties to find obstrns at 6.30 pm after a short only had been made.	
	11/1/18		Work continued on bury. 600 yds more bury and cable put in & trench recovered in for job from BEAUMETZ night & day parties at work from BEAUMETZ end.	

51st (Highland) Divisional Sigal Coy any R.E.   JANUARY 1918

Sheet 2.

Army Form C. 2118.

WAR DIARY
or
INTELLIGENCE SUMMARY.
(Erase heading not required.)

Place	Date	Hour	Summary of Events and Information	Remarks and references to Appendices
FREMICOURT	12/1/18		Work continued in laying 400 yards more laid & covered in & 400 more laid 500 yards more trench dug - night & day parties working for BEAUMETZ-ex Front test point	
	13/1/18		commenced. Cable laid down to top of Brigade Signal Dugout.	
			On on 12th 1st test pt completed & Laid dug to 400 yards E. of Bruno Mill	
	14/1/18		Night relief working parties stopped. Party of 100 field in trench to Bruno Mill	
			2nd test pt started. Cable laid in a LOUVERVAL dug to 80 yds S. Corps party.	
	15/1/18		Brigade test point completed. 2nd intermediate test point completed & third commenced. Very	
			severe snowstorm all day. Sig. dug 6ft 0 in am read ns with reference to relief. Preparatory	
			orders issued. Diagrams etc. Artillery following brn fried. scheme of R.A. communicated	
			to battr. O.P. Exchanges at pistol shells of Regt Battalion HQ & right Brigade (J17 & J25)	
			and at D26 C3.4. Rings being laid for each battery, Brigade & O.P. to R.A. artillery &	
			Captain Bruce of work. 152 Relief 15 & 3 Bde	
	16/1/18		Work on R.A. system with in preparation	
	17/1/18		Sig. Party to advance party pushed to ACHIET le PETIT to prepare D.H.Q. telephone 7 & Bde (J6 1/2)	
			Infy relieve 154 Bde. 152 Bde march to FREMICOURT to ACHIET advance party & D.H.Q.	
	18/1/18		152 Bde at ACHIET. Connected to IV Corps Signals to Div phones, no wires, Diagrams etc issued. No	

57th (2nd London) Divisional Signal Coy RE TF.   JANUARY 1918.   Sheet 3.

WAR DIARY
or
INTELLIGENCE SUMMARY.

Army Form C. 2118.

(Erase heading not required.)

Place	Date	Hour	Summary of Events and Information	Remarks and references to Appendices
FREMICOURT	19/1/18		Staff Guard to Havrincourt crosse GHQ. Sig Stores to ACHIET work Stores being extended by Divl transport.	
	20/1/18		Stores being extend to ACHIET.	
ACHIET le petit	21/1/18		DHQ moved to ACHIET LE PETIT 12 noon. Sig. A. wing L Army Signal Establish Signal School opened by Capt G Langford. OC Sigs	
			Le Calos 153 Bde to SAPIGNIES 15th Bde to IRLES × 3rd Bde as before	
			Hopkins attempt suffer laid on.	
	22/1/18		Work in power cable	24/1/15 30 A Sigs. B.Os. cable inspected
	25	11/15	Work on .... Bde to I...... of D.M.E	
	30/1/18	30/1/18	Work in camp. Training.	

J Minton
Major
OC 57th (2nd London) Sigl Cy RE
TF.

CONFIDENTIAL
No. 21 A
HIGHLAND DIVISION.

51 D Signals Vol 32

51st (H.) Divnl. Signal Co. N.C.(?)

War Diary

February 1918

1/fm
3/18

51st (HIGHLAND) SIGNAL COY RE TF — WAR DIARY — FEBRUARY 1918

Army Form C. 2118.

WAR DIARY or INTELLIGENCE SUMMARY

(Erase heading not required.)

Instructions regarding War Diaries and Intelligence Summaries are contained in F.S. Regs., Part II. and the Staff Manual respectively. Title pages will be prepared in manuscript.

Place	Date	Hour	Summary of Events and Information	Remarks and references to Appendices
ACHIET LE PETIT	1/2/18		Civil [?] for Cov relief [?] G.O.C Bhe visits [?]	
	2/2/18		152 Bde [?] received Bns [?] to Ablaincourt. Cable laid Bn to Div [?] [?] cable & [?] station	
			Cancelled [?] 153 Bde R.E carry [?] to Cnfn [?] [?] [?] Bn. Hdqs [?]	
			[?] Muddy weather [?] Bn Sections.	
	3/2/18		Muddy weather. HQs sect. 4/2/18. 5/2/18. 6/2/18 Coy on exercise. 7/2/18 – 8/2/18 Work nightly	
			in Camp. 9/2/18 Inspection of whole Coy (except RFA Bde section) by G.O.C. Presentation of medals	
			ribbons to Sjt Martin, 2/cpl Riddoch, 2/cpl Taylor & 2nd [?] Bealor, L/Cpl Trant. Sapper [?] Kerr, Pt. Gibson & Cordell	
			after Hunt & M.S.M. ribbon to Sjt Stair. 10/2/16. Exercise between parties & [?] units of 51st Div. & Bde.	
	11/2/18		Advance party of signalmen [?] to Fremicourt area, & exchange of [?] party [?] by 6th Divl. Sig.	
			152 Bde move to Fremicourt. 153 Bde line (left sector) 12/2/18 152 Bde line [?] [?] taking over
FREMICOURT	13/2/18	11.50am	D. HQ opened at FREMICOURT. 154 Bde to Fremicourt. All telephones etc installed. Lines	
			in area in very bad state, owing to destruction of overhead cable & [?] a fortnight before.	
	14/2/18		Weather harsh [?] cold. DX-MO Inspected Sigtry. 230 men employed [?] of [?] unfinished star J7.c.9.9.	
			Digging trenches below hut [?] as [?] [?] [?]	
	15/2/16		263 men & sigs a left Coy. Inspected sigt trny. Work on last position & roads for extreme front	
			centres on [?] cable laid to 174 Bde [?] [?] Kitchen, latrines & remaining at all stations & office	
			Bde section [?]	

51st (Highland) Signal Coy RE TF (1)

WAR DIARY
or
INTELLIGENCE SUMMARY.
(Erase heading not required.)

Army Form C. 2118.

February 1918

Place	Date	Hour	Summary of Events and Information	Remarks and references to Appendices
FREMICOURT	16/2/18		2:50 men continuing work on Offr lines. Every other man repairing DX M O route and 8 men on VU B2 route. BN Cable section still work on trip system in Offr & right B2 breezes.	
	17/2/18		Work on Offr lines continued & opn began toward Offr Bde. Work continued on DX M O & VU B2 routes. Horse had hoof shells finished. Visual station established betw'n from Bdes to Bdes Bdes. Transport ok Aldriant visiting Horse & Delsaure transport wire there & from DDDD made up from forward work at Delsaure will very certify moved up to new platform at Puisieux. OC Coy went to course at Athuries today.	
	18/2/18		Offrs & man Employed as above, at Delts to Coll'd wires. 2 PM & 4 PM guns overaged visual working Delsaure	
	19/2/18		In work on busy today owing to change of Bde in line. General Cable in Offr Bde area collected. Ratn DX M 0 and L - B2 repaired.	
	20/2/18		Shells for visual transmitting sts finished over Bull Rd Station Cable Selvery continued 152nd Bde relieved in 153rd Bde Sect by 154th Inf Bde	
	21/2/18		Relief of 152nd Bde by 154 completed this morning. Roubtin Station continued from wires titled up & southern Steel Panels Caulann 6.7 Pm. wires led to Art Offr	
	22/2/18		Party of 250 again at work on Offr lines.	

51st (Highland) Signal Co. R.E. T.F.

WAR DIARY
INTELLIGENCE SUMMARY

February 1918

Army Form C. 2118.

Place	Date	Hour	Summary of Events and Information	Remarks and references to Appendices
FREMICOURT	23/2/18		Work continued to left buried. Improvement of camp thro' lines continued.	
	24/2/18		Work continued to Left Bury.	
	25/2/18		D⁰.	
	26/2/18		D⁰. Pure Buzzer amplifier installed at Bn. H.Q.s. sick of DEMICOURT.	
			Unit's battery to DOIGNIES.	
	27/2/18		Left Bury completed to NINE ELMS & filled in. Testing cable as turned to various pairs.	
	29/2/18		In cable bury past tidy any to retire Part I Division with R.E. appear buried. OO to ground.	

J. Nicholson Capt.
51st Divn Signal Co. R.E. (T.F.)

51st Divisional Engineers

WAR DIARY

51st SIGNAL COMPANY R.E.

MARCH 1918

WD 33

Confidential

War Diary

March 1918

51st (H) Div. Sig. Co. R.E.

51st (Highland) Signal Co. R.E. (T.F.)   March 1918   (1)

Army Form C. 2118.

WAR DIARY
or
INTELLIGENCE SUMMARY.
(Erase heading not required.)

Place	Date	Hour	Summary of Events and Information	Remarks and references to Appendices
FREMICOURT	1/3/18		In bury party today took procedure in test points. New RE Pole Hqrs joined up with Beaumetz Bde preparatory to 3 Bdes being in line. New Hqr pole route keep on L to BZ. Detained with for 6 weeks course to Army Signal School at P.A.S.	
	2/3/18		140 new working troughs with Capt Bruce at upper end of L/eff bury making changes onto 2 arty OPs. Work continued of L-BZ tapp pole route adj artys pole ground cable VU-137. Bury	
	3/3/18		Work on EL proof so near end of L/eff Bury and 160 ft test point. Party of 60 men working on continuation of bury for Beaumetz back track & temp wires	
	4/3/18		Work on L-BZ & VU-137 continued also on test point & concentration. 140 with party continues 2 test pts 15 NE & OO continues	
	5/3/18		Party of 60 mls continued work in gallery. 140 with party continues. L/eff bury being tested. 2 pr/pa pole route continued. 2 tapple route continued. bush party of 60 in my Hd bury continues. Hd pr in Hqr exch of L for exchange. Galgin continued to NE + OO + testing	
	6/3/18		Work continued on tapp pole route & buries as before. New hut finished for LB test point	
	7/3/18		Work on NE + OO continued	
	8/3/18		Shelling from E pole Rd into L test point & Happald route from L-BZ finished. Right bury continued. Short route run from Rt Bde Hqr to join 6 tapp bury at J28 C3. 2 No alternative	

57th (Highland Div) Signal Co RE(TA)

Army Form C. 2118.

WAR DIARY
or
INTELLIGENCE SUMMARY

March 1918

Place	Date	Hour	Summary of Events and Information	Remarks and references to Appendices
FREMICOURT	8/3/18		Wrote to Right Batt'n of the Brigade near DEMICOURT. A complete installation of power amplifiers and rods for watchlights on June front as follows.— PB+ Amplifiers at J17A 5·6, J18D 4·9, J3+2·5, Power Buzzers J.5A 6·7, J.5D 2·8, K.7A 2·4, K.7D 9·9, D.28 D 9·8. Linned Wireless Sets at J.20 C 5·7 + I.12 D 3·3.	
	9/3/18		Capt J. J. Smith + Capt Brown at 6 AM under bombardment into our bivy opens from Coll head of Left Bivy the "Clover" Arty O.P. Remainder of party 175 in number continued Rifle bivy under the Lieutenant work on L tel front.	
	10/3/18		Party of 30 all under J Smith at 6 AM continued and also at NE, + OC, + BZ test points. Work on L tel front continued. 50 m p.m. Signal School and 1/100 Inf continued the Right bivy at Lair'oulh 440 yd length. Cpt Taylor + Cpt Laird & Wacrew + FTMO wrote to form bivy to NE, broke L test point continued & down at O.C.	
	11/3/18		NE test point bivy fitted and Hebes set. Frid 440 Junction Bay Rod. + BZ tery fitted up. L tel point forward exchange bivy fitted up.	
	12/3/18		Cable test out bivy set up.	
	13/3/18		Work on Aruna continued during the part to install power Jahns bivy finisher. Right bivy continued between BZ L'oubout L BZ Cord bivy fitted quite close. Right Ley Sgt Stan + Cpl Duy	

"51st (H) Divl Sigl C.R.P.T."

Army Form C. 2118.

WAR DIARY
or
INTELLIGENCE SUMMARY.
(Erase heading not required.)

March 1916

Place	Date	Hour	Summary of Events and Information	Remarks and references to Appendices
SOUASTRE	28/3/16		Div. moved to LA HERLIERE	
	29/3/16		Divn. moved to Henribette & three extensions from thence to Lilliers accompanying Divisl	
	30/3/16		Div. "HQrs" established at Louguenesse. Bishops line picked up & Cct to Police	
	31/3/16		surrounding villages. In 1st Corps. 1st Army.	

D. Cathlin Capt
for O.C. Signals
51st (H) Divl Sigl Co.

51st/Divisional Engineers

WAR DIARY

51st DIVISIONAL SIGNAL COMPANY R.E.

APRIL 1918

Attached:- Report on Communications
9th to 14th April 1918

WAR DIARY
or
INTELLIGENCE SUMMARY.

Army Form C. 2118.

21st (Div. H.Q.) Divisional Signal Coy R.E.
April 1918

Place	Date	Hour	Summary of Events and Information	Remarks and references to Appendices
Fouquières	1/4/18		Nothing of interest to record. Division in rest area with H.Q. at Fouquières.	
	2/4/18		Nothing of interest.	
Labourse	3/4/18		Divnl. H.Q. moved to Labourse & opened 11 AM taking over 3rd Div Fks. Bus from us at Fouquières. Bus B.Lys. on us to Labourse. Wire by Herts Lines.	
			153rd Bde closes 154th Auchel. CRA at Amette. CRE Labourse.	
	6/4/18		Route march for dismounted men. Storm & airplane experiences day out. Wilson Cope	
	7/4/18		Shoe sent round Bdes, which are completed with essential stores & kits	
Robecq	8/4/18	11.30 am	D.H.Q. opens Robecq. Bdes in truck. Under XI Corps.	
	9/4/18	4.15 am	Heavy Bombardment on XI & XV Corps Fronts. Enemy attack 55th Div & Portuguese. 55th Div in cave Paligues who retire thru' them.	
			154 Bde under 53 Div. 152 Div move to Zelobes, communication via L.Co. 153 Bde moves to Pacault.	
		1.0 pm	Bugle Cable run Robecq to Pacault. Single cable run back to Pacault to Robecq. A detach'd. No 1 Section T and W.T. set set up at D.H.Q. in windmill Cafe left of St Quentin Van Pacault.	
		3 pm	First line Horse Tramp to Pacault, second line thro' 7 pm. No 3 Section running pair from Pacault to 152 Bde at Zelobes.	

57th (H) Div. Sigl Coy
R.E.

WAR DIARY
or
INTELLIGENCE SUMMARY.

April 1918. Sheet 2

Army Form C. 2118.

Place	Date	Hour	Summary of Events and Information	Remarks and references to Appendices
ROBECQ	9/4/18	5p.	LCO move fm HINGES to ROBECQ. 53rd Div. at HINGES.	
	10/4/18	4.0am	152 Bde Join 153 at PACAULT. 155 to 253 Bde connected to PACAULT.	
		5.5a	154 Bde came under 57 Div. Sgt Shaw & C det. proceed to PACAULT to lay line betw. 152 & 154 Bde at LOCON. 152 network with Bdes by telephone, 153 by vival.	
		6.5a	Wired D.D. Sigls to Wilson Sgt.	
		9.5a	Cpl W/T set at QUENTIN close. Trench set sent out to PACAULT	
		10.5a	D.D. Sig. wires Wilson not beg'nent.	
		10.45am	10 mile D2, 10 mile D3 trickey sent to 152 Bde for distribution Bdes 3 Bdes. 20 line switches being installed in office. Rea Group of also established at HAM-en-Antrin.	
		11.30am	Line tkg fm 152 to 154 at LOCON.	
		12.50pm	Through to Wireless D.H.Q - 153 - PACAULT	
		3.45p	Wagon sent out to lay trickes fm D.H.Q to PACAUT.	
		4.0pm	C det laying line fm PACAUT to MEURILLON where 157 Bde (57 Div) will join them up giving lateral 153 to 157 Bde	
		5.15p	W/T station (AFB) sent up to 154 Bde HQs by lifting.	

Army Form C. 2118.

51st (H) Div: Sig: Coy April 1918
WAR DIARY
or
INTELLIGENCE SUMMARY. Sheet 3
O.E.T.
(Erase heading not required.)

Place	Date	Hour	Summary of Events and Information	Remarks and references to Appendices
R.O.B.E.Q.	10/4/18	6.45pm	Cable pair through to 152 Bde.	
		3.45pm	Cable pair through to 153 Bde.	
	11/4/18	6.15am	152 & 153 Bde HQs known not to be at LE CORNET MALO (Q.27.a.5.6.) A.S.S. M/T station outside to retire there. Arrangements made to cut wire last pairs.	
		6.30am	D.G.O. started, ready to move at D.H.Q. 7.45am sent to assist Bde in switching lines in event of new HQ.	
			Captain Bruce goes to Bde to lay a ground wire to R.A. Bde HQs.	
		8.30am	Wired A.D.S.G. (MD138) proceed to Catacombs for head of Sch.	
		9.15am	Through to new HQs of Bde on telephone pair.	
		9.25am	Arrived by A.D.S.G. that cable was on its way (30 miles).	
		10.0am	"A" detach. ordered to lay a pair R.O.B.E.Q. to 61 HQs at BUSNES.	
		10.15am	Capt. Sutherland sent out to clean of outstanding LE CORNET MALO.	
		10.45am	Visual communication with Bdes. (152 & 153) from R.O.B.E.Q. MILL to Bde HQs.	
		11.0am	Through to A.S.S. (152 & 153 Bde M/T station).	
		11.15am	10 miles D.7, 10 miles D.3 & 10 mile D.2 cable arrived from Corps.	
		10.15am	Through to 152 Bde line both relais avoid DA though to Corr. Q.A. exchange via 2 each relais	
		11.30am	51st Div. 181 Bde reported — to have 1 section MG Bn line 2 Coys in	

51 Div. Sig. Coy KET.   April 1918
                          Sheet 4.

WAR DIARY
or
INTELLIGENCE SUMMARY
(Erase heading not required.)

Army Form C. 2118.

Place	Date	Hour	Summary of Events and Information	Remarks and references to Appendices
ROBECQ	1/4/18	12 noon	C det. orders to lay pair ROBECQ to LES HARISOIRS (W.3.a.2.2) with 2 mins Cy galt with line & retirement of 154 B'de. S/o 154 Bde informed.	
		12.25 p	D. det. moved back from 152 Bde HQs; GDMG Captn Sutherland at cabin De HQs.	
		12.45	61 Div moved from BUSNES – "A" detach. ordered left line or C.H.A. exchange & visit to notes (MD158)	
		12.50 p	Dec to 154 Bde – WT unit – message received by W/T to effect that line lists to L'Epinette cable	
			Wagon to PONT L'HINGES: 1.45 p. Through again.	
		2.0 pm	Through from ROBECQ to XI C.H.A. BUSNES. Wagon (A detach) ordered back to ROBECQ. Reconnoitres HQs about (?) 26 D 5 3. Line will be cut to temporary HQs if necessary.	
		3.0 p	Cable wagon (B detach) at LES HARISOIRS: 4.0 p. advised that S/o 152 & 153 Bdes will fall back to W 11 C 2.2,	
			see 6 B 20 a 4.8, and that 154 will fall back to W 11 C 2.2.	
		4.5 p.	Cen line of Dz next to W 11 C 2.2, to be picked up by 159. to detach. at Post L'Hingue W 4 C 4.5, 1949 pm	
			to W 11 C 2.2 "A" detach. back in Camp.	
		5.0 p.	Through to W 11 C 2.2, & in touch with Bde lines. B detach ordered to return to ROBECQ.	
		6.0 p	B detach – ordered to Q 25.75 q to meet Captn Sutherland to provide for probable retirement of 152, 153 Bdes	
			& "A" det. include.	
		6.40	C detach. returned –	

Army Form C. 2118.

WAR DIARY
or
INTELLIGENCE SUMMARY

51=(H) S.J.W.G. (RETD)

April 1918.
Sheet 5.

(Erase heading not required.)

Instructions regarding War Diaries and Intelligence Summaries are contained in F. S. Regs., Part II. and the Staff Manual respectively. Title pages will be prepared in manuscript.

Place	Date	Hour	Summary of Events and Information	Remarks and references to Appendices
ROBECQ	12/4/18	5.30 a.m.	Enemy bombarded 152 & 153 Bde HQs having previously though in the darkness No 2 Section killed a captain with escaphita of 1 Sgt & 6 men & the remainder who broke through the German wounded station to No 3 Section success in capping. Lt 2 Divisional officers, 2 notnoydks, a both Sgts No 3 section killed, captured. Enemy surrounded Bde HQs while B.G.C. was talking telephone to 5th Seaforths, who stated 20 spirit the Second on the front!	
		7.30 am	BHQ moves to farm N. of BUSNES. Sgnl office opens at ROBECQ. W/T communication with 5154 Bde afterg one way to have of BH, & instruction begunents for G & both that line use out & the list mounting	
		9.0 am	Divl Rebeg station closed a relays in the live Yeaf to BUSNES to Capt. Hugh 61 Divn & XI Corps HQ transport & calls set sent to HAM.	
		12.30 pm	office opened at HAM for miscellanean Divl details.	
		3.0 pm	253 Bde RFA & 12 Australian Bde patrol RA Cmd. artB users, 153 Bde W L'ÉCHETTE line thys to 253 Bde at LA PIERRIERE & liven line Usires to 61 D HQ at L'ÉCOLE	
		6.0 pm	Head of S.Wrad.Line but thy to Emergency Fwd water GRE 5eDn & Robecq Cernel & Robecq Liair land 9 (Fleming Fred) with HQs at Robsen Cernel	

D. D. & I.L., London, E.C.
(A7883) Wt. W20/M1672 350,000 4/17 **Sch. 52a** Forms/C/2118/14

570/(H)Sgd Gy RF1.

Army Form C. 2118.

April 4/16.   Sheet 6

WAR DIARY
or
INTELLIGENCE SUMMARY.
(Erase heading not required.)

Place	Date	Hour	Summary of Events and Information	Remarks and references to Appendices
BUSNES	12/4/18	7.0p	B det. No 1 section with detail HQ & No 5 Section from Div. Sgd. Section lines run at 6.2h.	
		10.0p	CRA moves to 72c (61 Div HQ). DA Exch left at BUSNES, all brigades being in t. comm. to CRA via 258 Bde. HQ Sig. cable to form a line for BUSNES to MOLINGHEM.	
			R CRA now available if his retirement line.	
	13/4/18	9.30a	Second fair run to Pernes. Free Party sent to 70BEQ Gradie as cable available.	
			154 Bde relieve 6 BUSNER Pereches by B. De of 4th Div.	
			Line fit through L 6 - 177 & 182 Bdes. GRA. 3 to 154 Bde in BUSNES.	
		4.6p	2nd fair (via HAM) put through to XI Corps. Pair put to k BUSNES to MOLINGHEM.	See Diagm
			CRA holds HQ at MOLINGHEM.	
			fair run HAM to MOLINGHEM & for MOLINGHEM to BETTQUETTE, picking up Cofs of same	
	14/4/18		for BUSNES 154 Bde Comn with 61 Div. W/T set left with team	
		1.30p	D.HQ clos BUSNES opens at LAMBRES. Pam put through at HAM & FERGUETTE.	
			heavy 2 pr for CRA to "RA" astn Exchange at BUSNES one pair 61 Div (to MOLINGHEM)	
			to 154 Bx & one fr. 154y Bde to RA ad. Exch. at BUSNES.	
			Casualties the battle 9-14th April. Unnan: Lieut G. CUMMING (No 2 Section.)	
			Killed :- 2, Missing 24.	

51st (H'land) Div Sgn'l Cy R.E.   April 1918
Army Form C. 2118.

WAR DIARY
or
INTELLIGENCE SUMMARY.

Sheet 7.

Place	Date	Hour	Summary of Events and Information	Remarks and references to Appendices
LAMBRES	15/4/18		Clearing up. "D" detach'd. BRA HQrs. Sect. remain at BUSNES under Captain Bruce.	
	16/4/18		Starts bike's checking of store	
	17/4/18		No 2 section returned from No 5 section & HQrs. Lieut Laws takes over Command.	
	18/4/18		Work in Camp.	
	19/4/18		Work in Camp.	
NOEUX LES FONTES	20/4/18		D.HQ. moves to NOEUX LES FONTES.	
	21/22/4/18		Routine work in Camp	
	25/4/18		Divisional Signal School enrolled at ROMBLY under 2nd Lt Clarkson, 10 per section, 20 per Company.	
	26/4/18		Capt. R.A. ALLCARD R.E. joined the Company as second in Command.	
	to 30/4/18		Work in Camp, checking equipment, painting wagons etc.	

R Allcard Capt R.E.
for O.C. 51 (H) Div Signal C. R.E.

51st (H).Divisional Signal Coy.R.E.(T).

Report on Communication.

9th. to 14th.April 1918.

On the 8th.of April Divisional Headquarters moved from LABEUVRIERE to ROBECQ. Communication to all three Bgdes.and to Divnl.Artillery was established via Corps Exchanges. Two circuits connected the Division to the 11th.Corps at HINGES.

9th.April.
---------- On the advance of Bgdes.towards the River Lawe, the following communications were established:-

152nd.Bgde:- A circuit from HINGES was put through to Bgde.Hqrs.at ZELOBES,and on the retirement of the Bgde.to R.29 Central this circuit was again picked up.

Lines were laid by No.2 Section of the Signal Coy.to the 5th.& 6th.Seaforths near ZELOBES and to 6th.Gordons in ZELOBES. These battalions ran out lines to their Coys. These lines held practically without interruption.

153rd.Bgde:- Communication was established from Div.Hqrs.by Wireless to the Corps wireless station at QUENTIN,in anticipation of the move of this Bgde.forward.

A cable detachment of No.1 Section of the Coy.ran out a single cable line from ROBECQ to PACAULT (*),and ran a second line on the return journey. The Bgde.was in touch on the first line at 3 p.m. and on the second at 7 p.m.

No.3 Section connected their Bgde.Hqrs.with 152 Bgde.by a cable,and established touch by visual with 6th.& 7th.Black Watch and 7th.Gordons. Lines were subsequently laid to these Btns.by No.3 Section.

154th.Bgde:- This Bgde.moved to LOCON and was connected to HINGES 55th.Div.in this village. On the retirement of 55th.Div.to HINGES,the Bgde.was connected to HINGES by an existing circuit. No.4 Section laid out lines to the 4th.Seaforths,4th.Gordons & 7th.Argylls,and these batts. laid out lines to their Coys. Little trouble was experienced on these circuits.

10th.April. During the night 255th.& 256th.R.F.A.Bgdes.were connected to 153rd.Bgde.Exchange at PACAUT,and at 4 a.m. 152nd.Bgde.moved back to join 153rd.Bgde. A second circuit was laid from R.29 Central to PACAUT by No.2 Section and touch was maintained with the Bttns.of 152 Bgde.by telephone.

The Corps wireless station at QUENTIN closing at 9 a.m. a Divisional Trench Set was sent up at this hour to 153rd.Bgde.Hqrs.and maintained touch with a trench set at Divisional Hqrs.ROBECQ.

The following circuits were laid during the day by the cable wagons of No.1 Section.
    1 pair 152nd.Bgde.to 154th.Bgde.HQrs.at LOCON.
    1 pair 153rd.Bgde to 151st.Bgde.(50th.Div.) behind MERVILLE.
    1 pair D.H.Qrs.to 152nd.Bgde.

One of the single cables laid on the 9th.was given to the C.R.A.and an Artillery Exchange established at PACAUT,into which,lines from 255th & 256th.Bgdes were run.

In the afternoon a Divisional trench set was sent by car to 154th.Bgde.HQrs.and touch gained by wireless with this Bgde.from D.H.Q.

10 miles/twisted D 2 cable for the Infantry Bgdes.,and 10 miles twisted D 3 cable for the Artillery Bgdes.was sent up at 11 a.m. to PACAUT and distributed.

A Wilson wireless set was obtained from the Army and installed at D.H.Q. at 2 p.m.in place of the trench set up till then in use.

All surplus stores were sent back to HAM-EN-ARTOIS during the forenoon.

Bgde.to Battalion lines and R.F.A.Bgde.to Battery lines were altered as necessary during the day,by the Bgde.Sections concerned.

11th.April/contd.

(2).

11th.April:— 152nd.& 153rd.Bgde HQrs.moved back to L.E.CORNET MALO
The neccessary arrangements were made,and all communication re-established at 10 a.m. The Wireless stations moved back with their 153rd.Bgde. Captain Sutherland supervised the arrangements for the Infantry Bgdes.,and Captain Bruce for the R.F.A. Bgdes.

A Divisional Visual station was established at LE CORNET MALO working back to the mill in ROBECQ. A few messages were sent. The station was withdrawn at dusk.

A cable pair was run back to BUSNES to allow for a retirement of D.H.Q., and was temporarily connected to 11th.Corps H.A. Exchange at BUSNES.

In the afternoon a pair was laid to W.11.C.2.2. to meet 154th.Bgde on their retirement to this position. Touch was obtained with the Bgde.at 5 p.m., and later in the evening the Bgde.W/T set regained touch with the Division from this point.

In the evening all arrangements were made for a possible retirement of 152nd,153rd,255th,& 256th.Bgdes.to LES BAQUENOLLES FARM, and lines were diverted to run through this point.

30 miles of cable was received and distributed to 154th Bgde.and No.1 Section during the forenoon.

12th.April;— At 5.30 a.m the enemy rushed 152nd & 153rd.Bgde.HQrs.
The situation report for 152nd.Bgde.was received at 5.27 a.m.and quarter of an hour later both Bgdes.were found to be dis. Mounted linemen sent out,met the Brigade Major of the 153rd.Bgde.on the CALONNE ROAD and returned with the news.No.2 Section was captured with the exception of the transport and 6 men who escaped with most of the Bgde.Section Signalling Equipment. No.3 Section lost both Sergeants of the section. The operators at the wireless station succeeded in escaping with the entire equipment.

At 7.30 a.m.D.H.Q.moved to a farm west of BUSNES.
The line laid on the 11th.from ROBECQ was extended and lines were picked up from the 11th.Corps,61st.Div.and 11th.Corps H.A.
The Headquarters transport of the Coy.and one cable detachment moved to HAM,and opened a Signal office there at 12 noon for details of the Division,and to meet a further retirement.

An office was kept at ROBECQ till 9 a.m.and touch kept with 154th.Bgde.through it until Bgde.HQrs.moved back behind HINGES.

In the afternoon circuits were laid to 255th.,256th and 12 Australian Artillery Bgdes.,and R.A.Exchange opened at BUSNES. A liasion line was laid from 256th.Bgde.(LE PIERRERIE) to 61st D.H.Q. W of ST VENANT. A line was laid from BUSNES to 153rd.Bgde.at L'EPINETTE.

In the evening a scratch Bgde.section under Lieut.Laird was formed from No.1 Section to supply Flemings Force with signallers.

The circuit from BUSNES To ROBECQ was diverted to the HQrs.of this force (P.22.C) and lines run out to Btn HQrs. A wireless station was installed at the HQrs.of the Force.

13th.April A second cable pair was run to Flemings Force from BUSNES, a pair run to the 177th.& 180th.R.F.A.Bgdes.east of the canal, was A circuit put through from BUSNES to MOLINGHEM, while the C.R.A.retired at 4 p.m.

All cable and telephones dumped at ROBECQ and the vicinity by the 11th.Corps were salved and brought back to BUSNES, and the five R.F.A.Bgdes.refitted with cable.

14th.April. A cable pair was run from HAM to MOLINGHEM and another from MOLINGHEM to BERGUETTE.

On the withdrawal of the Division,the R.A.exchange was left at BUSNES,and two circuits put through from the C.R.A.to it by means of the above lines. A third circuit was put through from MOLINGHEM (61st Div.) to 154th.Bgde. The R.A.HQrs.section and one cable detachment remained at BUSNES.

The Coy.suffered the following casualties:—
Officers; Lieut.G.Cumming No.2 Section, Missing.
O.R.s Killed; One.
    Missing; Twenty
    Wounded; One
    Missing beleived Killed; Two.
There was little loss of equipment though a few telephones etc.were lost at LE CORNET MALO on the morning of the 12th.

Communication/

Communication presented little difficulty, and lines held up well throughout. The cable wagons were invaluable and wireless also did good work - e.g. after 9 a.m. on the 12th. no attempt was made to use anything else between 154th. Bgde. and the Division.

The flat and enclosed nature of the country rendered visual difficult, but 153rd. Bgde. used it with success on the 9th. & 10th.

There was some difficulty caused by the moving of the Corps Wireless D.S. without allowing for a second set to take up the work of the station while on the move. Difficulty was experienced in maintaining touch by Wireless with the 50th. Division which was working on a different wave length. Better liaison between the Armies concerned seemed needed.

No attempt was made by the Corps to provide lateral communication to the flank Divisions. Responsibility for this communication which is of great value, should be emphasised. A Divisional Signal Coy. has lateral communication between Brigades to provide for, and cannot deal with inter-division lines quickly.

Pigeons were not used as all forward lofts had been moved.

Owing to the uncertain state of affairs M.G. communications were by despatch rider. It is hoped in future to provide a separate telephone system, as equipment & personnel have now been obtained.

J. Muirhead.

Major R.E.

28/4/18.   O.C. 51st (H). Divisional Signal Coy. R.E.(T).

51st Division. G.

Herewith report asked for, regarding operations 9th – 14th April 1918.

J.S. Muirhead
Maj RE
O. 51st Signal Coy
RE.

28/4/18.

F.G/ 629.

DIAGRAM AT 1pm 10/4/18
All FnA Points are south of...

255 NFA B3e
256 NFA B2e
ZOD
Lyon
Front
208
W
ZOC
PACHU
WIN
YEA-TAR
YEE
LEO

YEA DIAGRAM 11.15am. 11/4/18

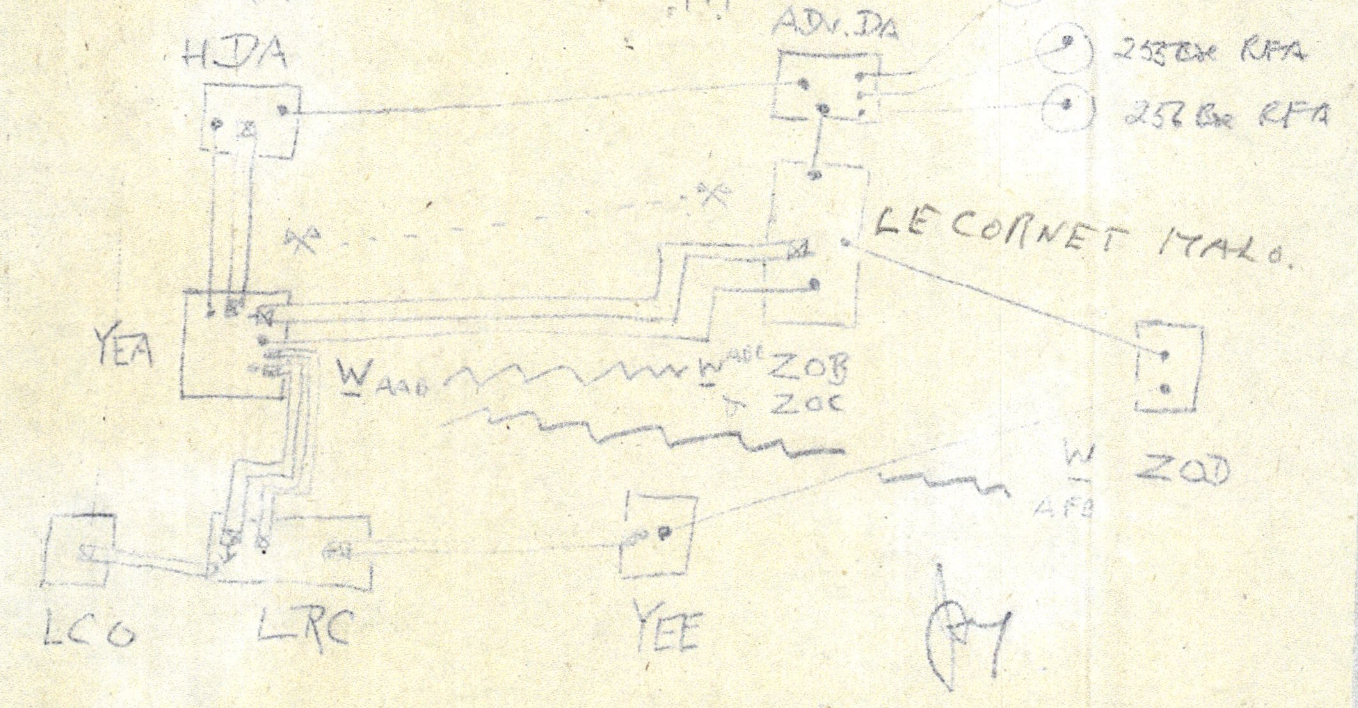

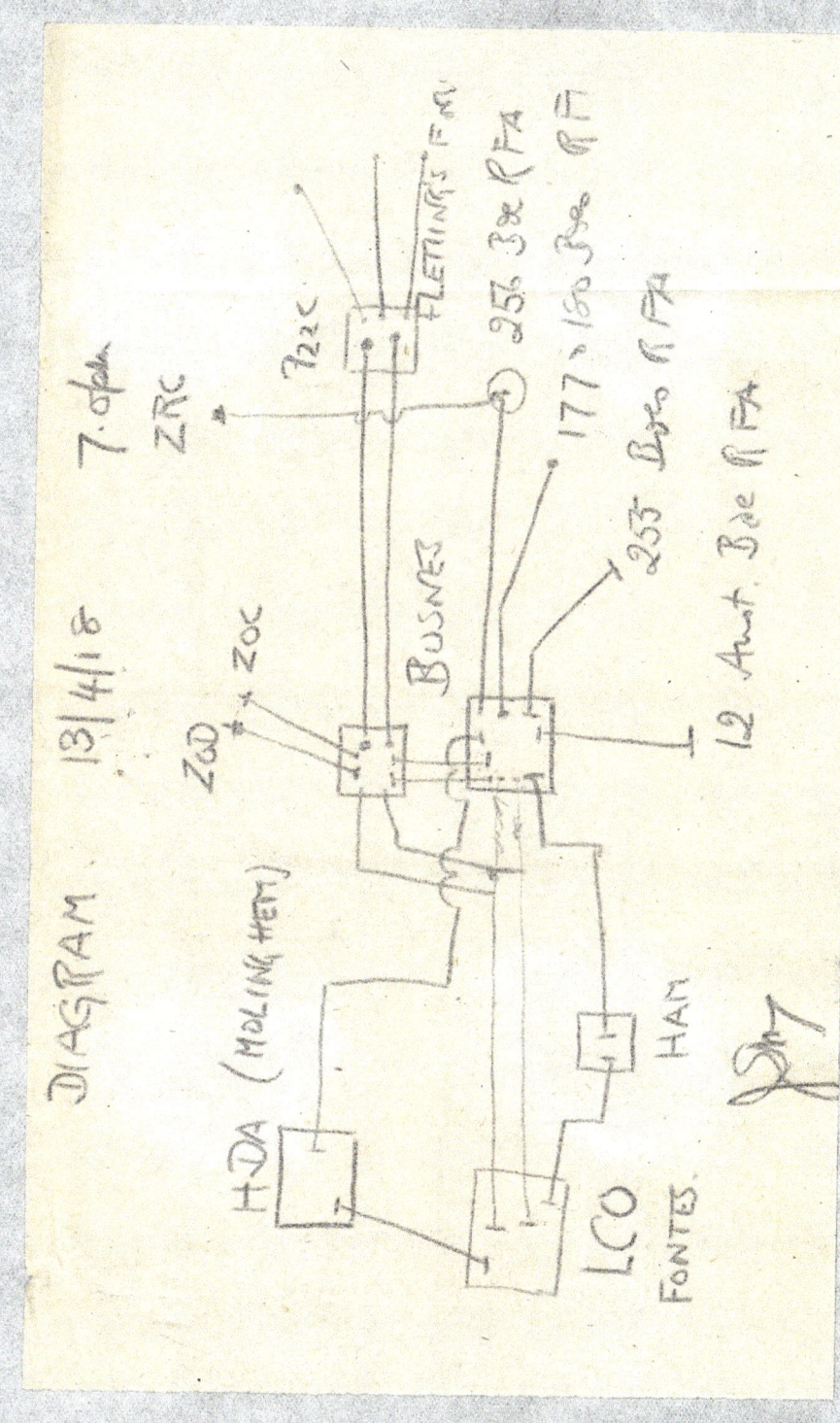

Confidential
Wd 35/Wa

War Diary
of
51st (H) Div. Signal Co. R.E.
for May. 1918.

51st Highland Division
Signal Coy R.E.

Army Form C. 2118.

WAR DIARY
or
INTELLIGENCE SUMMARY.
(Erase heading not required.)

May 1918. Sheet 1.

Place	Date	Hour	Summary of Events and Information	Remarks and references to Appendices
NORRENT FONTES	1/5/18 to 3/5/18		Work to Capt. Jacksons wagons etc. 4 letter code calls in use midnight 3rd/4th.	
	4/5/18		Advance party of linemen & operators under Lt. GAULDERE by lorry to MARŒUIL to prepare signal office in new sector.	
	5/5/18		Horse transport by road to DIVION, remainder of company train and lorry to MARŒUIL. 153 Bde in line under 4th Canadian division.	
MARŒUIL	6/5/18	9 a.m.	MARŒUIL less one relief. Close down at NORRENT FONTES, open at MARŒUIL. Division in XVII Corps, 1st Army. 152 Bde takes over line under 4th Canadian Division. Forward exchange taken over from Corps Signals at HSX test point A 27 a 6.2 sheet 51b. Code name AVENUE. 154 Bde at ECOIVRES. Horse transport arrived MARŒUIL	
	7/5/18	6 p.m.	Take over from 4th Canadian Divl Sig Coy completed. All forward lines underground except first 2000 yds which are permanent. Signal School at HAUTE AVESNES.	
		6 p.m.	154th DA move signal office from Aux RIETZ to MARŒUIL, 154 Bde to ECURIE Lt CURTIS joined the company	
	8/5/18		Testing at old bury RUINED FARM to AB test joint, cable nags two pairs to RP Divisional boundaries readjusted, 152 Bde at A 22 d 9.2, 153 remain at THELUS	

51st Highland Division
Signal C.R.E

Army Form C. 2118.

WAR DIARY
or
INTELLIGENCE SUMMARY.
(Erase heading not required.)

May 1918   Week 2.

Place	Date	Hour	Summary of Events and Information	Remarks and references to Appendices
MAREUIL	9/5/18	6 am	153 Bde moved to NINE ELMS A17 d Brouvrech cable laid out for new Hqrs	
	10/5/18		Party of 800 from 154 Bde on new laid cable route R.F. to M.C. Instruction in M.T. Lorry	
	11/5/18		Working on new Hqry. 11 pm 154 Bde relieved 153 Bde	
	12/5/18		300 men from 153 Bde on new Hqry	
	13/5/18		300 men from 153 Bde complete Hqry, 153rd Bde moved to [illegible] at 3.30 pm 6.30 RE & G	
			YEAR went from HSx to RR 5.30pm Signal School moved to CLIFF CAMP BRAY	
	14/5/18		Made a Hqry 152 Bde move to MB, H1d 3 2	
	15/5/18 16/5/18 17/5/18		Made a Hqry, testing out old Hqry AB & Co. R.F, repairing old position near A3 Continue work on Hqry and fitting in panels. 10.30 pm 153 Bde relieved 152 Bde [?]	
			CURTIS temporarily I/C signals of 153 Bde	
	18/5/18		Rival of ground cables to R.F, 14 pairs now though on Hqry	
	19/5/18		Church Parades	
	20/5/18 21/5/18		Completing ground lines 1 pair 6 pr 8 am 21st to 8 pm 23rd all telephone communication failed. - Divisional area swept supposed on position. In the open 6 pair trunk cable laid from BL Cct put to BR for new position left 2/f Bde.	
	22/5/18			
	23/5/18	9.30pm	152 Bde relieve 154 Bde at new H.Q. B3, 14 & R2, 153 Bde now 6 Bde H.Q. all left Bde H.Q. 154 Bde into reserve at ECURIE	

51st Highland Division
Signal Co. R.E.

WAR DIARY or INTELLIGENCE SUMMARY
(Erase heading not required.)

May 1918 Sheet 3

Army Form C. 2118.

Place	Date	Hour	Summary of Events and Information	Remarks and references to Appendices
MARŒUIL	24/5/18		Relay of out-going power cable	
	25/5/18			
	26/5/18		Check parades, marching orders issued, kits inspection by O.C. Motor ch.	
			Returned unit, Lt LAIRD takes over signal school at GODDARD temporary to 153 Bde	
	27 to 28/5/18		Overhauling waggons, testing cable	
	29/5/18		154 Bde relieve 153 Bde in right sector	
	30/5/18		Lt CURTIS reforms HQ La GAMME-2 returns to 153 Bde	
	31/5/18		Buzz or to OB right Bde cut by shell, two temp. lines laid in running pair finally repaired by 6.20 pm	

R. Allard. Capt. R.E.
for O.C. 51 (H) Div. Signal C.R.E.

Confidential

War Diary
of
51st (H) Div. Signal Co. R.E.
for June, 1918

Vol 36

WAR DIARY   JUNE 1918

51st High. Divnl Signal Coy R.E. T.F.

51st. Highland Divison Signal C.R.E.   June 1918   Sheet 1.

Army Form C. 2118.

WAR DIARY or INTELLIGENCE SUMMARY.

(Erase heading not required.)

Instructions regarding War Diaries and Intelligence Summaries are contained in F. S. Regs., Part II. and the Staff Manual respectively. Title pages will be prepared in manuscript.

Place	Date	Hour	Summary of Events and Information	Remarks and references to Appendices
MAROEUIL	1/6/18		Moving horses & holding near camp for which company establishing Capt. MACDONALD	
	2/6/18		"K" Corps Signal Co. temporarily attached to the Company	
			LT CURTIS taken over command 152 Bde Section & Capt. Mc MACDONALD temporarily 153 Bde section	
		3.0pm	6.5.45pm heavy to left Bde but this cut by shellfire	
	3/6/18		Coy. Extended visual cable to P.d. C.P. post	
	4/6/18		153 Bde relieve 152 Bde in Left sector	
	5/6/18		Work on rear amb & layout line for hrs hors shot	
	7/9/6/18		Work on buzzer test & new arty.	
	10/6/18		152 Bde relieve 154 Bde in right Bde sector	
	11/6/18		Routine works rebuilding A.B. test point, clearing funk hs D.W.R.R.	
	12/13/6/18		Moving W/T station O.V. to O.C. Lt. GODDARD to 153 Bde Section vice Capt. MACDONALD rejoined x Corps	
	14/6/18		154 Bde relieve 153 Bde in Left sector	
	18/6/18		51 Div Arty relieved 15 Div Arty. D detachment refrom H.Q	
	19/20/21/6/18		Routine work	
	22/6/18		153 Bde relieve 154 Bde in Right sector	
	23/6/18		Lt Gallway to hospital, Lt. GODDARD to 154 Bde Section	

51st Highland Division Signal C. R.E. June 1918

WAR DIARY or INTELLIGENCE SUMMARY.

Army Form C. 2118.

Sheet 2.

Place	Date	Hour	Summary of Events and Information	Remarks and references to Appendices
MAREUIL	24/6/18		Routine work, reeling up cable in front line trenches.	
	to 24/4/18			
	27/4/18		Lt CUTBUSH to 153 Bde, Lt GAMMELL resting at H.Q. about 76 all ranks of the company suffering from P.U.O.	
	28/6/18		152 Bde relieve 154 Bde in Left Sector.	
	29 and 30/6/18		Laying of forward wires, burying cable BR to BE.	

R Allcard. Capt. R.E.
for O.C. 51st Div. Signal C.R.E.

Divisional Engineers,

51st (Highland) Division.

51st DIVISIONAL SIGNAL CO., R. E.,

JULY, 1918.

Vol 37

Confidential

War Diary

of

51st (H) Div. Signal Co. R.E. T.F.

for July. 1918.

51st Highland Divis'n Signal R.E.   July 1918

WAR DIARY
or
INTELLIGENCE SUMMARY.

Army Form C. 2118.

Sheet 1.

(Erase heading not required.)

Instructions regarding War Diaries and Intelligence Summaries are contained in F.S. Regs., Part II. and the Staff Manual respectively. Title pages will be prepared in manuscript.

Place	Date	Hour	Summary of Events and Information	Remarks and references to Appendices
MARGUIL	1/7/18 to 3/7/18		Routine work.	
	4/7/18		154 Bde relief of 153 Bde in Right Sector	
	7/7/18		LT. LEWIS to 153 Bde section, LT GAMMELL to 152, LT CURTIS to 1st Army Signal Co.	
	8/7/18		Packing up, sorting stores etc. Preparatory to handing over lines to 4th Can. Div.	
	9/7/18		153 Bde to CHATEAU de la HAIE.	
	10/7/18		Preparing new office at ROLLECOURT. 152 Bde to ECURIE	
ROLLECOURT	11/7/18 7pm		Office at MARGUIL closed 12 noon on relief by 4th Can. Div. Opened at ROLLECOURT 7pm. 152 Bde to DIEVAL, 154 to ANZIN.	
	12/7/18		153 Bde to FOUFFLIN-RICAMETZ 154 to ORLENCOURT, Main line to Latter place, other lines provided by Army Signals	
	13/7/18		153 to CHELERS, Artillery still in line, infantry stand not / Bgs well. Warning orders, prepare to entrain. Packing mags etc.	
	14/7/18 6pm		Company proceeds to BRYAS and entrain there, leaving at 6.0pm	
NOGENT sur SEINE	15/7/18		In train all day till 10.0pm, ordered suddenly to detrain at NOGENT sur SEINE. Company bivouacs in field near the town.	

Army Form C. 2118.

WAR DIARY
or
INTELLIGENCE SUMMARY.
(Erase heading not required.)

July 1918 Sheet 2

Place	Date	Hour	Summary of Events and Information	Remarks and references to Appendices
VILLENAUXE	16/7/18		Company proceeds to VILLENAUXE. Absorbed men by French Corps Wireless Estbn.	
ST. PRIX	17/7/18		Transport leaves VILLENAUXE 6.30 am. arrive SEZANNE 11.0 am, marches on to ST. PRIX. 2.45 p.m. till 6.30 p.m. 32 Riders in all O.C. trip at MOUSSY with mounted personnel.	
MOUSSY	18/7/18		Leave ST. PRIZ 10.30 a.m. via MONTMORT to MOUSSY arrive 6 p.m. 22 Riles.	
HAUTEVILLERS	19/7/18		To HAUTEVILLERS at 11.0 a.m. under XXII Corps. Orderleys Net not suggested for attack next morning, lines to Corps advanced at and Italian exchange C.W. set from Corps. W/T forces for W/T communication 6 Corps. A DET Lt. LAIRD, B DET Lt. WILSON opened out at 7.30 p.m. to lay lines ST. IMOGES to Brigades.	
ST. IMOGES	20/7/18		Div. Advanced H.Q. at ST. IMOGES, Bdes in BOIS DE COURTON, Clear dawn and sun all over HAUTEVILLERS to XXII Corps at 6.0 a.m. ZERO at 6.0 a.m. 153 on left 154 Bde on right 152 in reserve, 62nd Div on right, 9th French on left attack progress well. Lines held of fairly well. all earth return.	
	21/7/18		YEAR opened on BOIS DE COURTON at 7.0 am, 152 Bde attacked at 8.0 am. Progress well. Niagara have now laid 30 mls of D.III Union direct & thro' YEAR to 153 & 152 Bdes in BOIS de COURTON 154 Bde at NANTEUIL.	

Army Form C. 2118.

Instructions regarding War Diaries and Intelligence Summaries are contained in F.S. Regs., Part II. and the Staff Manual respectively. Title pages will be prepared in manuscript.

WAR DIARY
or
INTELLIGENCE SUMMARY.   July 1918   Sheet 3

(Erase heading not required.)

Place	Date	Hour	Summary of Events and Information	Remarks and references to Appendices
ST. IMOGES	22/7/18		Infantry still pushing on but not much change in communications.	
HAUTVILLERS	23/7/18		152 Bde to NANTEUIL, then closes down ST IMOGES at 2.0 pm, reopens at HAUTVILLERS.	
	24/7/18		New lines are laid and metallic circuit & communication reopened, YEAR at NANTEUIL — ST (crow roads)	
and 25/7/18			153 Bde at ST. IMOGES in reserve, new signal office at D.H.Q.	
	26/7/18		154 and 153 Bdes change positions, lines poled and repaired for previous attack. 153 Bde and YEAR own	
	27/7/18		Division attacks again with success, many returns rapidly.	
NANTEUIL			at to NANTEUIL valley. DIV gun NANTEUIL 6.0 pm.	
	28/7/18		Infantry and Brigades continue to push on. 60th regen lay lines to CHAUMUZY, and ESPILLY, Adv of Mtd gd BOIS DES ECLISSES and MONTAGNE DE BLIGNY, regen ordered back at dusk.	
	29/7/18		YEAR regained at MARFAUX, line laid ESPILLY to CHAUMUZY, Infantry to move out of line.	
	30/7/18		153 Bde in reserve at NANTEUIL, Artillery begins to come out.	
CRAMONT.	31/7/18		All Bdes to NANTEUIL, open office CRAMONT, transport arrives 5.30 pm, handover to 14th French division, closed down office closed down NANTEUIL at	
		10.0 pm	one line to civil exchange at CRAMONT.	

R Wilcocks Capt R.E.
o.c. 51 Div Signals R.E.
for

'O'. 51st.(H).Division.
A.D.Signals, XXIIth.Corps.

Herewith as requested, Report on Communication during the
operations 20th. - 29th.July 1918.

(signature)
Major R.E.
O.C.51st (H).Divisional Signal Coy.R.E.(T).

Copy to Director of Signals,
G.H.Q.

51st.(H).Divisional Signal Coy.R.E.(T).

Report on Communications during operations in the
Valley of the River Ardre 20th.- 29th. July 1918.

Signal communications in these operations presented no novel features.

All means of communication were employed - cable, visual, wireless, pigeon, motor cyclist, mounted orderly and runner - and previous experience as to their employment in semi-mobile warfare was confirmed.

There were certain difficulties of circumstance and country which at times rendered communication difficult, but with rare exceptions touch was maintained by telephone, up to battalions and batteries. The absence of detailed reconnaissance caused lines to be laid in places exposed to shell fire or traffic- faults which were difficult to rectify owing to the continual changes in the situation - and the wooded nature of the country militated against the success of the small wireless stations between Brigades and Battalions, while on the right the presence of the River Ardre hampered Power Buzzer communication.

The following lessons can be drawn:-

VISUAL

More use was made of Visual Signalling than previously. There is still a tendency however to seek cover for visual stations in open fighting. This is unnecessary legacy of trench warfare as the enemy is much too occupied to trouble about lamp stations in open country.

CABLE.

The correct method was employed in pushing up advanced exchanges from which short spurs can be laid to Brigade or Battalions. As a whole, considering the difficulties, lines held well, though in mobile conditions speech must always be precarious owing to Buzzer induction on earth circuits.

It should be understood that what chiefly prevents good line communication is divergence of HQrs. off the main line of advance. This necessitates the employment of the very few men available to run and maintain long spurs of cable, and indefinitely postpones improvements on the main forward lines. There are only at the outside 20 linemen available to lay and maintain all the lines of a Division, and at the outside 10 men per Brigade and there is a limit to what they can achieve.

SUPPLY OF CABLE.

This was exceedingly difficult as the Corps were not in a position to draw on large stocks, and there was no cable available at the outset except the small establishment total. Brigades were kept supplied, but Battalions were dependent very soon on what they could recover - providentially in several cases abandoned stocks of Italian cable were found and used. I consider that the whole question of of cable supply in battle needs consideration. There is no system in existence similar to that supplying ammunition and there is no doubt that if cable could be regularly supplied, it could time and again be advantageously used.

Every effort was made to keep the Artillery supplied and sufficient cable was carried forward to keep them in stock. All formations did their best to recover cable, and a certain amount was picked up and used again.

WIRELESS

Trench Sets again proved excellent and worked uninterruptedly between Brigades and Division, whenever erected. Unfortunately on the night of the 26/27th. the station at 152 Bgde.HQrs. could not be erected owing to the darkness, or else the temporary /

WIRELESS

temporary loss of touch with this Bgde. could have been obviated.

In several cases good results were obtained between Bgdes. and Battalions by means of Loop Sets and Power Buzzer & Amplifiers. This is their first successful employment by this Division in mobile fighting, and confirms the policy of keeping the Brigade Wireless pool permanently under the control of the Signal Coy.

The Loop Set is not however a very reliable instrument.

C.W.Wireless would have undoubtedly been of the greatest assistance to the Artillery, and it is to be hoped that instruments will soon be issued.

4. **PIGEONS.**

These were little used and times were rather slow. The birds were flown to French lofts.

5. **DESPATCH RIDERS.**

Mounted Despatch riders were of great use throughout and were freely employed.

At present only one motor cyclist can be spared per Brigade and two for the Artillery. One extra motor cyclist per Infantry Bgde. and one motor cyclist per Artillery Bgde. would be thoroughly useful in moving fighting.

6. **ARTILLERY COMMUNICATIONS.**

These followed the system previously employed, and proved satisfactory. The provision of a special circuit from the C.R.A. to the R.F.A. Bgdes. and the liaison officers at Infantry Bgdes., was again ensured throughout.

Visual was largely and successfully used in open country between Bgdes. and Batteries, and O.P's.

The establishment of Lucas Lamps however proved quite inadequate for the conditions met with and caused considerable difficulties. It is strongly urged that an establishment of 3 lamps per brigade and 4 per battery be authorised.

7. **M.G.BTN.COMMUNICATION.**

The Battalion Hqrs. were connected to the Divisional Exchange. M.G.Coys were connected to the nearest Bgde. exchange or to the Divnl. Advanced Exchange.

Telephone calls were necessarily slow as Divisional calls took priority but messages were sent by telegraph. Communication to Sections was mainly by runner, but in several cases Section Commanders were with Infantry Btn. Hqrs. and communicated with M.G.Coy.Hqrs. via Bgde. lines. Lamp was not successful owing to the wooded nature of the country.

---

8. **SIGNAL EQUIPMENT.**

Artillery Equipment has been dealt with above. I consider the present reduction of Battalion telephones to 3 D III telephones not justified, and would urge that the original scale of 5 be re-established as soon as supplies permit. The Lucas Lamp has supplanted all other visual equipment. Emphasis should be laid on the fact that flag should only be used for preliminary training, and that as soon as Signallers are at all proficient attention should be concentrated on the Lamp.

Fullerphones were not used owing to the doubtful nature of lines, and the need for as little equipment being carried as possible.

Major R.E.

10/8/18. O.C.51st (H).Divisional Signal Coy.R.E.(T).

WAR DIARY

51st (High) Divisional Signal Coy R.E. T.F.

for

August 1918

51st Highland Division Signal Co. R.E.
August 1918
Sheet 1.

FE/371
Army Form C. 2118.

WAR DIARY
or
INTELLIGENCE SUMMARY.
(Erase heading not required.)

Place	Date	Hour	Summary of Events and Information	Remarks and references to Appendices
CRAMONT	1/8/18		D.H.Q. at CRAMONT all day. Boches were from NANTEUIL to village near EPERNAY, also returned to extreme west day. Total casualties in company were July 20: officers nil, 2 o.r.s. died of wounds, 13 o.r.s. wounded in general, chiefly from Att. Bde. Subsections. Official report on communications to attached Juvencourt.	
	2/8/18 10 a.m.		Office closed at CRAMONT; Company entrained OIRY 8.0 p.m.	
	3/8/18		Company arrived PERNES by train about midnight.	
VILLERS-CHATEL	4/8/18		Office opened VILLERS-CHATEL 9.0 a.m. Bde. arrive during day 152 at CAUCOURT, 153 at CHATEAU de LA HAYE, 154 at BERLES. Artillery at AUBIGNY and take over existing lines.	
	6/8/18		In rest. Overhauling instruments and stores, practice in laying cable, flag drill etc.	
to	15/8/18			
MAREUIL	16/8/18		Company moved to MAREUIL, taking over from 52 (Lowland) Division 154 Bde. at O.E. 153 to Pernes (?) ACQ(?) I.N. north of SCARPE.	
	17/8/18		152 Bde. to ... F.R.G.3 BLANGY, 170 Bde. at River Lt. Bow. ARRAS.	
	18/8/18		170 Bde. at 1.0 p.m. operation south of Scarpe, 152 Bde. patrols in FAMPOUX during the night.	
	19/8/18			
	20 ...			
	21/8/18		Boche post forced into enemy front line.	

51st Highland Divnl. Signal Co. R.E.

Army Form C. 2118.

WAR DIARY or INTELLIGENCE SUMMARY.

August 1918. Sheet 2

Place	Date	Hour	Summary of Events and Information	Remarks and references to Appendices
MARCEUIL	22/8/18		170 Bde one unit of Corps held by XVII Corps Cyclists	
	23/8/18		Sector S. of SCARPE handed over to 3rd Can. Div., the division passing Canadian Corps.	
	24/8/18	4.30am	153 Bde successful attack on ZION ALLEY. Div. advanced exchange at LBX.	
	25/8/18	5.0am	capt'd HOARY, HAGGARD and NAVAL trenches.	
	26/8/18		Successful attack of Canadian Corps. 153 Bde supported by 154 Bde on left and 152 Bde	
			along the Scarpe also advanced towards GREENLAND HILL. 153 Bde moved to POINT DU JOUR	
	27/8/18		Further limited objectives taken. 159 Bde from MAISON BLANCHE, 152 to CAM VALLEY	
			DIV. ADVANCED to BLANGY. 'G' to VICTORY CAMP.	
	28/8/18		Div. H.Q. Rear and remainder of Signal Co. to VICTORY CAMP. 154 Bde move to	
			PEPPER TRENCH at H.16.d.1.8. 153 Bde into reserve at ROCLINCOURT.	
	29/8/18		Capture of GREENLAND HILL	
	30/8/18		Division comes under XXII Corps. Office at MARCEUIL closed down, work done on	
			old trunk lines forward to NZ East army railway	
	31/8/18		DIV. H.Q. all to VICTORY CAMP. Advanced exchange opened at BLANGY.	

Allard. CAPT. R.E.
for O.C. 51 Divn. Signal C.R.E.

51st.(H).Divisional Signal Coy.R.E.(T).

Report on Communications during operations in the
Valley of the River Ardre 20th.- 29th. July 1918.

Signal communications in these operations presented no novel features.

All means of communication were employed - cable, visual, wireless, pigeon, motor cyclist, mounted orderly and runner - and previous experience as to their employment in semi-mobile warfare was confirmed.

There were certain difficulties of circumstance and country which at times rendered communication difficult, but with rare exceptions touch was maintained by telephone, up to battalions and batteries. The absence of detailed reconnaissance caused lines to be laid in places exposed to shell fire or traffic- faults which were difficult to rectify owing to the continual changes in the situation - and the wooded nature of the country militated against the success of the small wireless stations between Brigades and Battalions, while on the right the presence of the River Ardre hampered Power Buzzer communication.

The following lessons can be drawn:-

VISUAL

More use was made of Visual Signalling than previously. There is still a tendency however to seek cover for visual stations in open fighting. This is unnecessary legacy of trench warfare as the enemy is much too occupied to trouble about lamp stations in open country.

CABLE.

The correct method was employed in pushing up advanced exchanges from which short spurs can be laid to Brigade or Battalions. As a whole, considering the difficulties, lines held well, though in mobile conditions speech must always be precarious owing to Buzzer induction on earth circuits.

It should be understood that what chiefly prevents good line communication is divergence of HQrs. off the main line of advance. This necessitates the employment of the very few men available to run and maintain long spurs of cable, and indefinitely postpones improvements on the main forward lines. There are only at the outside 20 linemen available to lay and maintain all the lines of a Division, and at the outside 10 men per Brigade and there is a limit to what they can achieve.

SUPPLY OF CABLE.

This was exceedingly difficult as the Corps were not in a position to draw on large stocks, and there was no cable available at the outset except the small establishment total. Brigades were kept supplied, but Battalions were dependent very soon on what they could recover - providentially in several cases abandoned stocks of Italian cable were found and used. I consider that the whole question of of cable supply in battle needs consideration. There is no system in existence similar to that supplying ammunition and there is no doubt that if cable could be regularly supplied, it could time and again be advantageously used.

Every effort was made to keep the Artillery supplied and sufficient cable was carried forward to keep them in stock. All formations did their best to recover cable, and a certain amount was picked up and used again.

WIRELESS

Trench Sets again proved excellent and worked uninterruptedly between Brigades and Division, whenever erected. Unfortunately on the night of the 26/27th. the station at 152 Bgde.HQrs. could not be erected owing to the darkness, or else the temporary

2.

WIRELESS

temporary loss of touch with this Bgde. could have been obviated.

In several cases good results were obtained between Bgdes. and Battalions by means of Loop Sets and Power Buzzer & Amplifiers. This is their first successful employment by this Division in mobile fighting, and confirms the policy of keeping the Brigade Wireless pool permanently under the control of the Signal Coy.

The Loop Set is not however a very reliable instrument.

C.W.Wireless would have undoubtedly been of the greatest assistance to the Artillery, and it is to be hoped that instruments will soon be issued.

4. **PIGEONS.**

These were little used and times were rather slow. The birds were flown to French lofts.

5. **DESPATCH RIDERS.**

Mounted Despatch riders were of great use throughout and were freely employed.

At present only one motor cyclist can be spared per Brigade and two for the Artillery. One extra motor cyclist per Infantry Bgde. and one motor cyclist per Artillery Bgde. would be thoroughly useful in moving fighting.

6. **ARTILLERY COMMUNICATIONS.**

These followed the system previously employed, and proved satisfactory. The provision of a special circuit from the C.R.A. to the R.F.A. Bgdes. and the liaison officers at Infantry Bgdes., was again ensured throughout.

Visual was largely and successfully used in open country between Bgdes. and Batteries & Batteries and O.P's.

The establishment of Lucas lamps however proved quite inadequate for the conditions met with and caused considerable difficulties. It is strongly urged that an establishment of 3 lamps per brigade and 4 per battery be authorised.

7. **M.G.BTN.COMMUNICATION.**

The Battalion Hqrs. were connected to the Divisional Exchange. M.G.Coys were connected to the nearest Bgde. exchange or to the Divnl. Advanced Exchange.

Telephone calls were necessarily slow as Divisional calls took priority but messages were sent by telegraph. Communication to Sections was mainly by runner, but in several cases Section Commanders were with Infantry Btn. Hqrs. and communicated with M.G.Coy.Hqrs. via Bgde. lines. Lamp was not successful owing to the wooded nature of the country.

----

8. **SIGNAL EQUIPMENT.**

Artillery Equipment has been dealt with above. I consider the present reduction of Battalion telephones to 3 D III telephones not justified, and would urge that the original scale of 5 be re-established as soon as supplies permit. The Lucas Lamp has supplanted all other visual equipment. Emphasis should be laid on the fact that flag should only be used for preliminary training, and that as soon as Signallers are at all proficient attention should be concentrated on the Lamp.

Fullerphones were not used owing to the doubtful nature of lines, and the need for as little equipment being carried as possible.

Major R.E.
10/8/18. O.C.51st (H).Divisional Signal Coy.R.E.(T).

WR 39

Confidential.

War Diary

of

51st (H) Div. Signal Co. R.E. T.F.

for

September, 1918.

WAR DIARY or INTELLIGENCE SUMMARY

Army Form C. 2118.

51st Highland Division Signal C.R.E.

September 1918   Sheet 1

Place	Date	Hour	Summary of Events and Information	Remarks and references to Appendices
VICTORY CAMP NORTH OF ARRAS	1 to 2/9/18		Work on old buried cable routes continues.	
	3/9/18		153 Bde relieves 154 Bde in PEPPER trench, 154 to ROCLINCOURT.	
	4/9/18 to 10/9/18		Nothing of interest during this period. Company engaged on usual maintenance work. Party of 1 officer and 26 men from 25th Div. Signal Company engaged in relaying cables, and testing out old bury south of SCARPE between MENCHY, NX bury continually carried under LT. BRIGGS of 475 Signal Co.	
	13/9/18		Relief by 492 Div. commences.	
MARŒUIL	14/9/18		Closed down at VICTORY CAMP at 10.0 am. Opened at MARŒUIL same time. 153 Bde at MONT ST ELOI, 152 DAINVILLE CAMP, and 153 Bde at CAMBLAIN L'ABBÉ.	
	15/9/18		During period of rest, Company engaged in overhauling stores, instruments, equipment etc. Calls detachments by practice calls. Reorganisation of Company regarding Officers takes place; Lt. GAULD takes over the Wireless section, 2/Lt WILSON to No 5 Section, Lt. MACGREGOR	
	16 to 23/9/18		to No 1 section 4 Lines, Lt. COUTTS to No 1 section, Lt LAIRD takes up an instructors appointment at BEDFORD. Division moves to prepare to relieve 4th Div. in the line.	
	24/9/18		Preparing to take over at VICTORY CAMP.	
	25/9/18		Closed down at MARŒUIL, opened VICTORY CAMP at 10.0 am. Brigades at CAM VALLEY and PEPPER TRENCH.	

51st Highland Division
Signal Co R.E.

September 1918
Sheet 2

Army Form C. 2118.

WAR DIARY
or
INTELLIGENCE SUMMARY.
(Erase heading not required.)

Instructions regarding War Diaries and Intelligence Summaries are contained in F. S. Regs., Part II. and the Staff Manual respectively. Title pages will be prepared in manuscript.

Place	Date	Hour	Summary of Events and Information	Remarks and references to Appendices
VICTORY CAMP	26/9/18 to 30/9/18		Comparatively quiet period in the line, near Livy to GREENLAND HILL sector. Cm wires not used to DIV. ARTY.	

Allcard Capt. R.E.
for OC 51 Div Signal Co R.E.

WAR DIARY
51st (H) Divisional Signal Coy.

October 1918.

WAR DIARY

51st Divisional Signal Coy

51st Highland Division
Signal Co R.E.

October 1918.

Army Form C. 2118.

WAR DIARY
or
INTELLIGENCE SUMMARY.

Sheet 1.

(Erase heading not required.)

Instructions regarding War Diaries and Intelligence Summaries are contained in F. S. Regs., Part II. and the Staff Manual respectively. Title pages will be prepared in manuscript.

Place	Date	Hour	Summary of Events and Information	Remarks and references to Appendices
VICTORY CAMP	1/10/18		Preparing to hand over to 8th Div.	
	2/10/18		Lt THOMAS attached from 1st Army Signal Co. R.E.	
CHATEAU	3/10/18		Closed down and rejoined CHATEAU P/ACR at 10 a.m. Intensive training of	
	4/10/18			
D/ACR	5 & 6/10/18		Intensive training of cable sections, counting and overhauling stores	
	7/10/18		Packing up & gear, stores etc	
INCHY EN ARTOIS	8/10/18		Company marched to QUARRY WOOD near INCHY EN ARTOIS, V.28.d.	
	9/10/18		Lt THOMAS posted to Company and taken over No 2 Section. 2nd Lt GAMMELL	
			Co. No 1 Section. Found about 6 cd. wagons, stores, transport not down to light scale.	
BOURLON	10/10/18		Company moved to cant. west of BOURLON taking over from 3rd CAN DIV.	
ESCADŒUVRES	11/10/18		Company moved to ESCADŒUVRES in preparation to taking over line to which Canadians	
			had advanced after capturing CAMBRAI. A & B detachts laying line to 152 & 153 Bdes.	
NAVES	12/10/18		Attack by 152 and 153 Bdes, a slight opposition, lines continued to IVUY where	
			Bdes advance to A & B detachts to remain forward. Cable down ESCADŒUVRES	
			– NAVES 5.0 p.m. Bde line diverted by A. Det. Cyclists C'list.	

51st Highland Division
Signal R.E.

October 1918

WAR DIARY
or
INTELLIGENCE SUMMARY.
Sheet 2

Army Form C. 2118.

Place	Date	Hour	Summary of Events and Information	Remarks and references to Appendices
NAVES	13/10/18		A & B Detchts at 1UWY. let line not extended officially, no return to E.Q. in memory a Det. left spare line to 1UWY.	
	14/10/18		YEAR opened at 1UWY. thing of cable necessary. Additional cables laid clear. Back permt road to 1UWY, but lines not	
	15/10/18		being out, while enemy the line is still going again. 15th Bde relieves 154 Bde.	
	16/10/18		Overloading began to prevent line to Bdes. Valley roads to enemy lines. 1UWY gave much trouble. There are 2 5" Bde Phones somewhere.	
	17/10/18		Work improving lines. CW station at MILLE AVESNES letter entirely (OP) what there to 3 SDA at 1UWY & DA. NAVES. 154 Bde relieves 152 in cyclet water, 152 botto in TILWY & MARTIN. Lines they for extended.	
	18/10/18		4 Pairs Cable from end of German Cut. about 2000 yds SE of 1UWY to a plan sunken road 1000 yds SW AVESNES LE SEC; 2 pair to(?) NAVES to German Permanent at Rly Jc. W of NAVES, & Pr from Junction of more to 157 Bde to AVESNES LE SEC.	
	19/10/18		2 pr laid fr DHQ NAVES to AVERNES LE SEC & 2 prs fr 1UWY (SF 24 8 D) AV LE S. Found Exch of old at AVESNES LE SEC. Etaing cable for fr of 2 pr can ones on Lft during the day, & delivered in every places	

51st (HIGHLAND) Div.
SIGNAL COY RETIF

OCTOBER 1916
Sheet 3

Army Form C. 2118.

WAR DIARY
or
INTELLIGENCE SUMMARY.
(Erase heading not required.)

Place	Date	Hour	Summary of Events and Information	Remarks and references to Appendices
NAVES	19/10/16		G. Div. Sectn.	
			B cable det. ran'd to 153 Bde Hq Y	
			Hq man. G LIEU ST AMAND to Div HQ at AVESNES. A det. ran'd from Y	
			to AVESNES HQ, seen as also 2 relief to inform DS. E det. order to	
			relief 153 Bde at AVESNES at 6 am to move fwd with Bde. A cable	
			from Div Trunk to NOYELLE S/R SELLE. 23.00. Tpy AVESNES G.BEV.	
	20/10/16	03.00	C det. sent fwrd to AVESNES, & layin fwrd to NOYELLE	
		05.00	B det. at AVESNES & laying to LIEU. 07.00. A det. laying to AVESNES, 08.30. E office	
			relief & inform DS. hare G AVESNES. Trunk G LIEU & NOYELLE 10.00	
AVESNES LE SEC.		09.00	D. HQ close NAVES, reopen AVESNES to SEC. Coy less Hqs transport G AVESNES to Hq B	
			to-day. 152 Bde at AVESNES, 153 at LIEU, 154 at PAVE de VALENCIENNES. Then to last C.L.	
			Line laid 153 Bde to 153 at LIEU, DA Hq at AVESNES. B/T N.R. Div G. Corps not of	
			Hqs. 18.37. 153 open DNCHY. Line extra from LIEU.	
do	21/10/16		Cav Corps AVESNES to 152 & NOYELLE returns to man Q.9. Par lais 152 G.DNCHY to Agt.	
			B det. laying line DNCHY to NOYELLE. C det. lay G. B" HQs at FLEURY, 3 pole line laid	
			yesterday, HQs transpd, B det. attacks from 11 Div S pole move G AVESNES, 11 Div det. poles	
			Line laid G A Bde this morning.	

51st (H) Div Sgnl Cy WD.

OCTOBER 1918.
Sheet 4.

Army Form C. 2118.

WAR DIARY
or
INTELLIGENCE SUMMARY.
(Erase heading not required.)

Place	Date	Hour	Summary of Events and Information	Remarks and references to Appendices
AVESNES LE-SEC	21/10/16		152 Bde move to DOUCHY 12.00 hrs & take over 153 Bde conc to C.	
			152 Bde clearge. D's Co Cable all day up to 14.00. 153 Bde HQ's.	
		Noon	151st Div move to AVESNES; later line jet thro'. P's Co cable to Ry Sta at NOYELLES.	
			Will ayle cable & poles. Lonposed to Cafe to collect cable.	
		18.00	Asst. exchange opened at NOYELLES in SERLE. 152 Bde in exchange. Full phone	
			superimposed. C det. lay cable during afternoon to fut. roads 1000 yds SE of THIANT (Company HQs). Line of Divisional front now on River Ecaillon. Enemy regains possession of THIANT. Loop into entry wire between 152 Bde & Battalions	
			lines poles AVESNES to NOYELLES & to DOUCHY. B det. lay line DOUCHY to 4th Can	
	22/10/16		Div Art to chabach DENAIN, 153 relieve 154 in the line, 154 to DOUCHY at noon	
			A & C detachments restabli ways & clearing up.	
	23/10/16	11	U Div Sct & C det. lay Dbin along railway btw fm AVESNES to NOYELLES. A det lamp 3 bain NOYELLES	
			to lay railway line DOUCHY to when. D wire Beforadts with ruston made Sr W. flank (I 2 requ. UT)	
			HQ line in full't throat German counter in direction of THIANT.	
	24/10/16	04.00	51 Div attack the line of R. ECAILLON. 153 Bde in the line, 152 MSY on outposts Stygd Co	
			take by 1000 & more lines to prominion reports. B & C dets resty by turnins exp syls	

51(H)Div Sgnl Coy RE.

OCTOBER 1916
Sheet 5.

Army Form C. 2118.

WAR DIARY
or
INTELLIGENCE SUMMARY.
(Erase heading not required.)

Place	Date	Hour	Summary of Events and Information	Remarks and references to Appendices
AVESNES le SEC.	24/10/16		in billets. kept German guns as yesterday, on HAULCHIN STATION. B Sect. laying	
			3 cables from HAULCHIN STATION to Fabrique de Bulow THIANT.	
		10.30	Run to Hyp over Lille below Douai & THIANT. H.Q Spur thing to THIANT.	
		17.30	152 Bde to NOYELLES, line extended to YEAR. B cable detail, shell-through killed 1 man killed,	1 man killed, 1 wounded.
	25/10/16	07.00	Attack renewed. Objective gained Enflade. A det. repair line to THIANT	
		14.00	152 Bde hve to THIANT. 153 Bde hve to Fque de Bouron's THIANT. Line extension	
			at NOYELLE as per diagram attached.	
	26/10/16		152 Bde move to THIANT – relieve 152 + 153 Bde. C set move to THIANT. A det. lay	
			line AVESNES to NOYELLES. Adv. Exch. closed at NOYELLES opened at THIANT.	
			153 Bde move to HAULCHIN Chateau, a line laying laid from to Adv. Exch to 153	
			& Cief. On wire work to J.A. Div H.Q. & R Bde in THIANT.	
	27/10/16		Manoeuvre. Reels up from NOYELLES to DIEPPE to DA.	
	28/10/16		152 Bde attack MONT HOUY crosses, captures all objective. Adv. party sent	
			to Beau ville de Boushain to fit up exchange etc. A det. lay a pair LEV SS	
			AMAND to Beau ville by Cable overland via AVESNES le SEC & Avup to Div	
			le Bde.	

57th (H) Divl. Sigal Cy R.E.   OCTOBER 1918.

WAR DIARY or INTELLIGENCE SUMMARY.   Sheet 6.

Army Form C. 2118.

Place	Date	Hour	Summary of Events and Information	Remarks and references to Appendices
BASSE VILLE de BOUCHAIN	29/10/18		Div relieved by 49 Div. DHQ opens at BOUCHAIN 10.00. A set. left at Divl HQ under 49 Div Sigs. Remainder of Cy to BOUCHAIN.	
"	30/10/18		Cleaning up.	
IWUY	31/10/18		DHQ move to IWUY CHATEAU. Cy move by road. 152 Bde G.T.W.in ST MARTIN. Earth return circuits run out to them. 154 & ESCADOEUVRES. 153 to HORDAIN. (opens 1/11/18) on relief.	

J Munteau
Major R.E.
O.C. 57th Sigal Cy R.E.

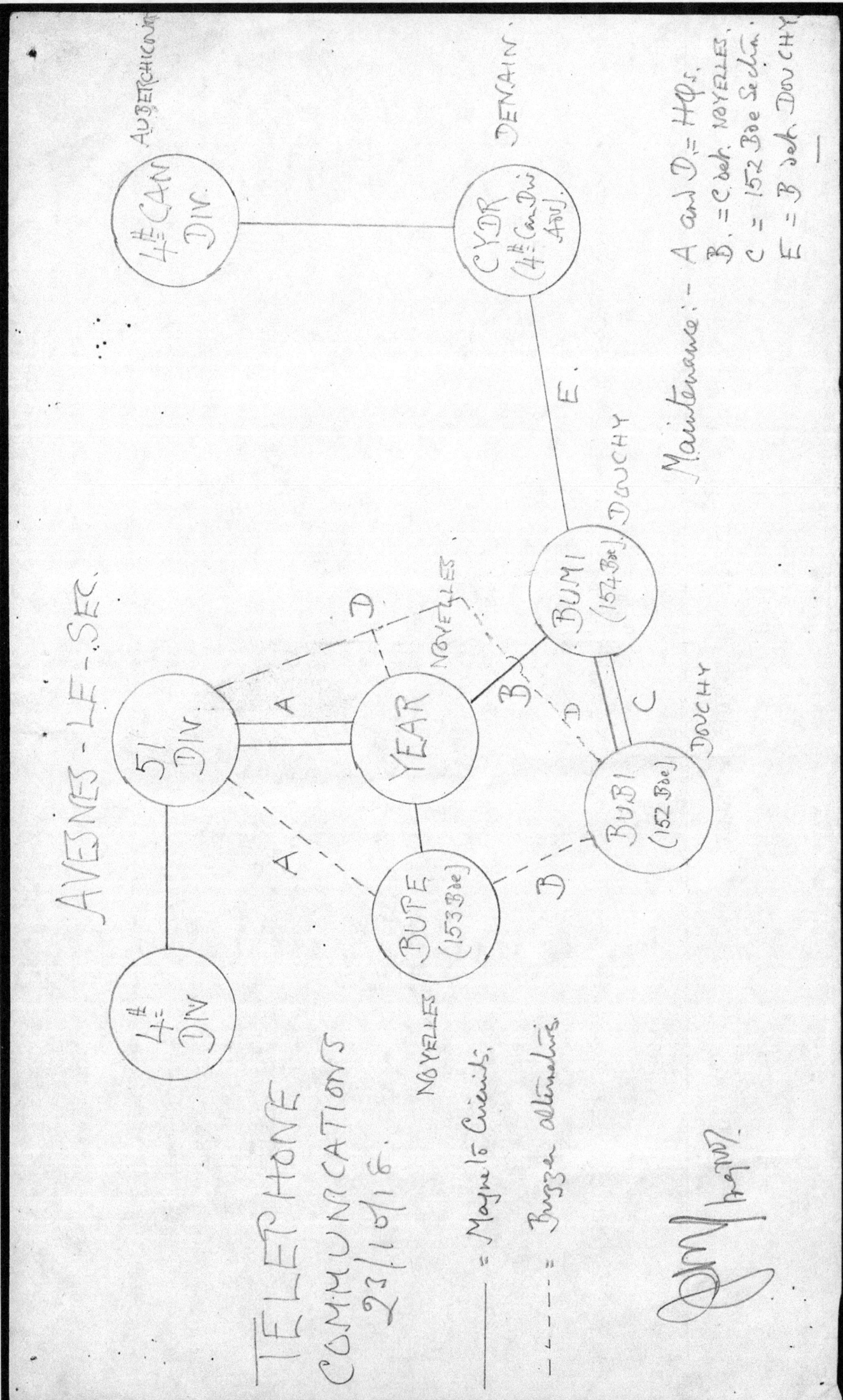

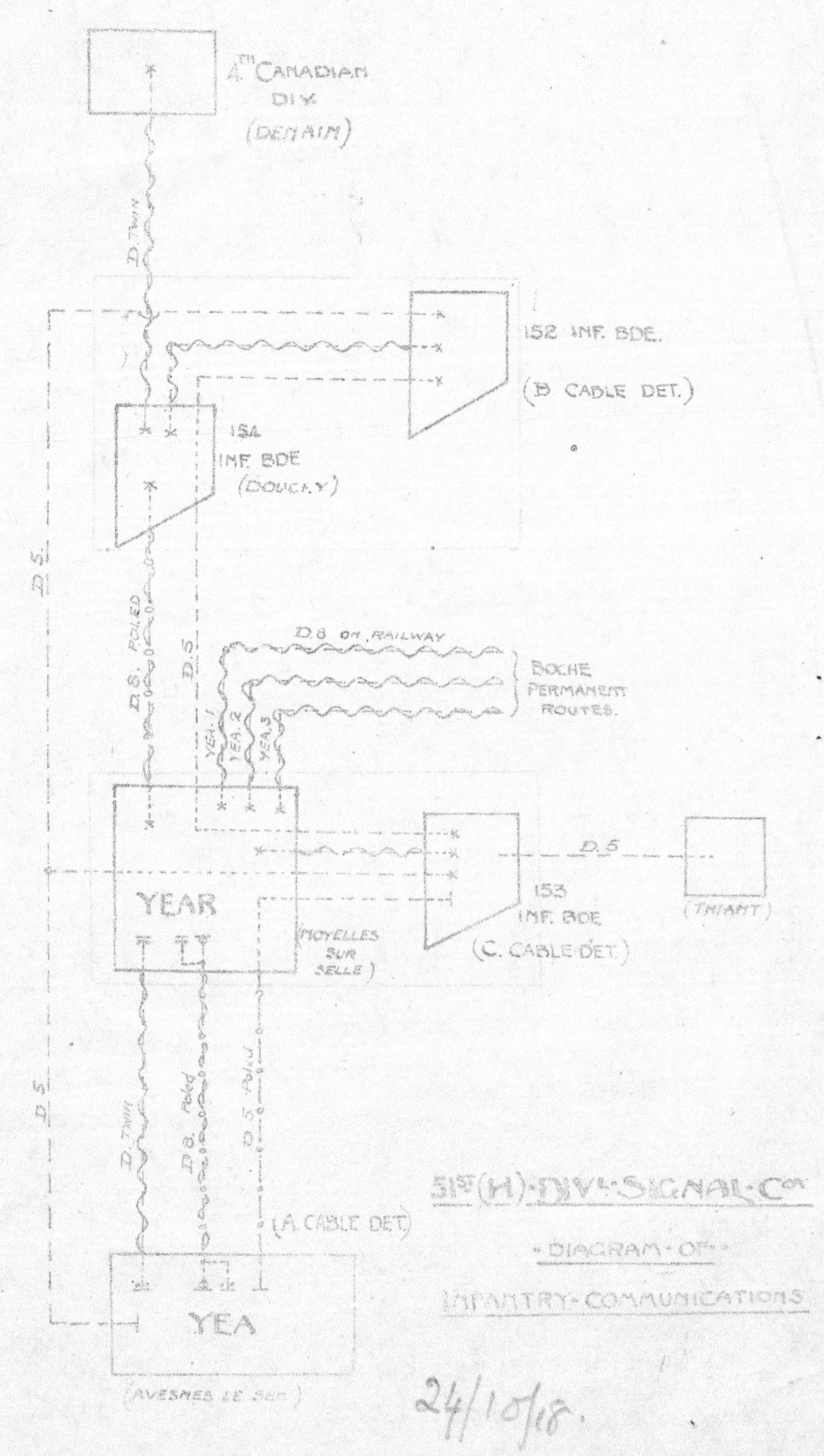

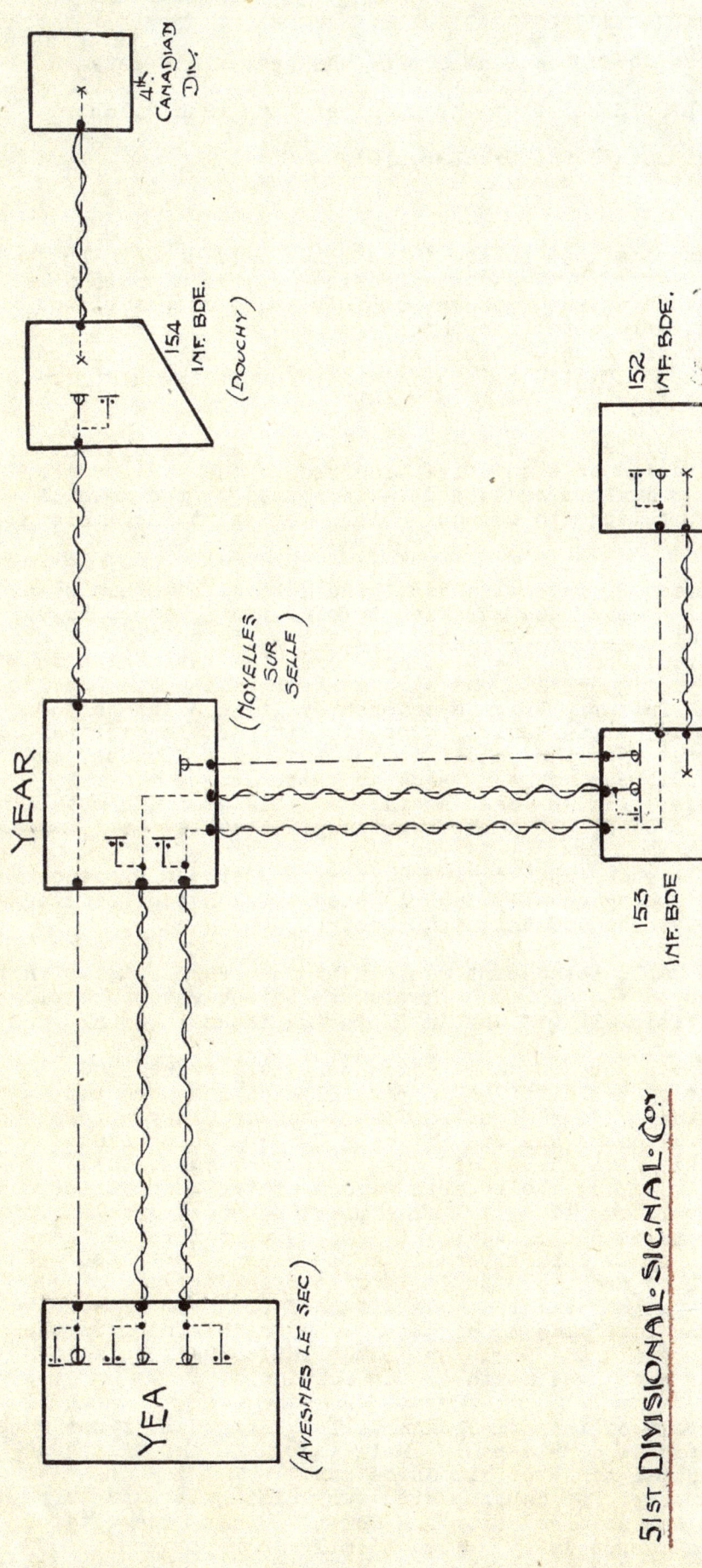

Nov 18

51st (H) DIVISIONAL SIGNAL COY. R.E. (T).

Report on Communications during the operations between CAMBRAI and VALENCIENNES from the night of 11th/12th.October to the night of 28th/29th. October, 1918.

I   Communications followed the lines laid down in 51st Div. G.322/116, viz: forward communication centres at which telephone exchanges, and, where possible, wireless stations were erected, were established forward of Headquarters of formations on the line of their advance. From these forward exchanges lines radiated out to inferior formations and formations on the flank.

II   This system worked well, and, with rare exceptions when concentration of enemy fire occurred in the vicinity of communications centres, or some delay occurred in the move of Headquarters, telephonic communications was maintained throughout the Division.

III   Between Divisional and Brigade HQs the same number of lines, as has in previous experience found best, was employed, i.e, two circuits from the Division to the Division Communication Centre, 2 circuits from the Division Communication Centre to each Infantry Brigade, and one circuit from each R.F.A. Groups direct to the Infantry Brigade covered by it, and one to the Division Communication Centre. One circuit was, in addition, provided direct from the C.R.A. to the two R.F.A. Groups, and a second circuit was added as soon as possible.
         These circuits were, as far as cable allowed, metallic, and, where run on single cable, were duplicated at the first opportunity.
         Fullerphone working was maintained between Division and Brigades, being usually superimposed through two transformers at the Division Communication Centre.

IV   One Cable Detachment was allotted to each Brigade in the line, and one to the C.R.A. The fourth Detachment was employed in wiring Divisional HQs', and in improving the main trunk lines forward.
         The two forward Cable Detachment, after they had completed the system detailed in para.II. and III., were put at the disposal of the Brigade Signal Officers to whom they were attached, and, on several occasions, ran the main Brigade Trunk Lines forward. These Detachments did most excellent work, the N.C.Os i/c frequently taking their cable wagons up to, and even beyond, battalion HQs in the line. The prevalent mist enabled this work to be carried out in daylight, and, except for one team which was hit by an unlucky shell, cable wagons were used with impunity well in front of the field batteries.
         One Cable Detachment was attached from the 11th. Divnl Signal Coy for lateral communication with the Division on the left, and connected the Division Communication Centres to the corresponding exchanges north of the Scheldt.

V   Forward of Infantry and Artillery Brigades, lines were maintained despite considerable shell-fire, and the telephone was the principal means of communication.
         The supply of cable proved very difficult, and very little cable was obtained from the Corps. This necessitated strict economy, especially as practically no replacements of the lighter types of cable could be counted on. The use of the cable wagons forward of Brigades saved light cable, and all units salved a considerable amount of cable, and used it again.

VI   Good use was made of Visual Signalling when weather permitted, but, for the most part, the ground mist prevented good visual work. Throughout the Division, however, the value of visual work is well appreciated, and it was used wherever practicable.

VII   Wireless proved of the utmost value.

(a) Infantry Brigade HQs were throughout in touch with the Division by wireless, and several hundred messages were sent without delay.

Pack ponies were used during the earlier stages to transport the sets at the Brigade HQs, but latterly all these animals became casualties, and, owing to losses among the Divisional sections, could not be replaced. In most cases, however, a limbered wagon was sent from HQ Section to move Brigade stations.

(b) Power buzzers and amplifiers were used with success from the 13th to the 16th from left Brigade HQs at IWUY to Battalion HQs. After this, distances proved too great, and these instruments, although they are reliable and easily get into touch with each other, suffer from jamming from earth return circuits, and are really legacies from trench warfare. They proved, however, valuable during the heavy shelling of IWUY.

(c) Loop Sets were throughout used with success between the Brigade HQs and Brigade Communication Centres or Battalion HQs. Two rear sets were usually employed to work to each other, and a range of 6000 yards was obtained. Messages came through expeditiously, and little jamming was experienced. The Brigade Pool of Signallers have now confidence in these sets, and can be relied on to obtain touch quickly, and deal with all traffic given them, without delay. Enciphering was done by Signal personnel, but a considerable number of messages, which gave no information to the enemy, was sent in clear.

(d) C.W. stations were used for the first time by the Artillery in moving warfare. Communication was maintained between D.A. HQ and Group HQs, but, owing to faults in the stations and the comparative lack of training of the personnel employed, working to O.Ps was precarious. A station in the water-tower at the Chateau at AVESNES LE SEC was, however, in touch with Group and D.A HQs during the 17th and 18th October.

The same difficulties as were met with in 1917 with Spark Wireless are at present being experienced with C.W. Wireless, but better instruments are now being issued, and the Artillery personnel, once it reaches the standard of the Divisional and Infantry Brigade Wireless Sections, will certainly repay the trouble required to train it. A good deal was learnt technically during these operations, and the comparative failure to ensure good C.W. communication does not affect the certainty that great use can, and will, be made soon of Artillery wireless.

(e) The Divisional charging plant was adequate to maintain the supply of accumulators, and all stations were throughout provided with requisite batteries, which were forwarded regularly from D.H.Q.

VIII   The condition of the roads rendered motor-cycles almost useless for a considerable period, and mounted despatch riders were used. If further operations occur this winter additional mounted men will be necessary for communication between D.H.Q. and Brigades, and C.R.A. and Artillery Groups. There are only 4 D.R. horses on the establishment of the Signal Company H.Qs, and no assistance can be obtained from the cable sections, as mounted linemen are also required by them. The Signal Officers' chargers were used, but, as Signal Officers require horses urgently on many occasions, this is a precarious source of supply.

IX   The grouping of Brigade and Group H.Qs close to
each other greatly facilitated communication. It is
important, from the point of view of communications,
that D.H.Q. should move in large bounds as was done in
these operations. Each move of D.H.Q. necessitated a
disproportionate expenditure of cable in local telephone
circuits, and the diversion of, at least, half of the
Divisional Sections from work on the main routes, and
intermediate positions of H.Qs. are a great waste of
labour and material.

J Muirhead.
Major R.E.

3/11/18.   O.C. 51st (H).Divisional Signal Co.

S.G.745/97.

152nd Infantry Brigade.
153rd Infantry Brigade.
154th Infantry Brigade.
C.R.A.
C.R.E.
1/8th Royal Scots.
51st Bn., M.G.C.
'Q'.
A.D.M.S.
Signals.

Please forward by November 7th reports on the operations between CAMBRAI and VALENCIENNES from the night of the 11/12th October to the night of 28/29th October 1918. Infantry Brigades will forward copies of Battalion accounts and tracings of dispositions on the evening after each attack.

1st November 1918.

Lieut-Colonel,
General Staff,
51st (Highland) Division.

51st (H) DIVISIONAL SIGNAL COY. R.E. (T).

Report on Communications during the operations between CAMBRAI and VALENCIENNES from the night of 11th/12th October to the night of 28th/29th. October, 1918.

I. Communications followed the lines laid down in 51st (H) Div. G. 322/116, viz: forward communication centres at which telephone exchanges, and, where possible, wireless stations were erected, were established forward of Headquarters of formations on the line of their advance. From these forward exchanges lines radiated out to inferior formations and formations on the flank.

II. This system worked well, and, with rare exceptions when concentration of enemy fire occurred in the vicinity of communications centres, or some delay occurred in the move of Headquarters, telephonic communication was maintained throughout the Division.

III. Between Divisional and Brigade HQs the same number of lines, as has in previous experience found best, was employed, ie, two circuits from the Division to the Division Communication Centre, 2 circuits from the Division Communication Centre to each Infantry Brigade, and one circuit from each R.F.A. Groups direct to the Infantry Brigade covered by it, and one to the Division Communication Centre. One circuit was, in addition, provided direct from the C.R.A. to the two R.F.A. Groups, and a second circuit was added as soon as possible.

These circuits were, as far as cable allowed, metallic, and, where run on single cable, were duplicated at the first opportunity.

Fullerphone working was maintained between Division and Brigades, being usually superimposed through two transformers at the Division Communication Centre.

IV. One Cable Detachment was allotted to each Brigade in the line, and one to the C.R.A. The fourth Detachment was employed in wiring Divisional HQs', and in improving the main trunk lines forward.

The two forward Cable Detachment, after they had completed the system detailed in para.II and III, were put at the disposal of the Brigade Signal Officers to whom they were attached, and, on several occasions, ran the main Brigade Trunk Lines forward. These Detachments did most excellent work, the N.C.Os i/c frequently taking their cable wagons up to, and even beyond, battalion HQs in the line. The prevalent mist enabled this work to be carried out in daylight, and, except for one team which was hit by an unlucky shell, cable wagons were used with impunity well in front of the field batteries.

One Cable Detachment was attached from the 11th. Divnl Signal Coy for lateral communication with the Division on the left, and connected the Division Communication Centres to the corresponding exchanges north of the Scheldt.

V. Forward of Infantry and Artillery Brigades, lines were maintained despite considerable shell-fire, and the telephone was the principal means of communication.

The supply of cable proved very difficult, and very little cable was obtained from the Corps. This necessitated strict economy, especially as practically no replacements of the lighter types of cable could be counted on. The use of the cable wagons forward of Brigades saved light cable, and all units salved a considerable amount of cable, and used it again.

VI   Good use was made of Visual Signalling when weather
        permitted, but, for the most part, the ground mist pre-
        vented good visual work. Throughout the Division, how-
        ever, the value of visual work is well appreciated, and
        it was used wherever practicable.

VII   Wireless proved of the utmost value.
            (a) Infantry Brigade HQs were throughout in touch
        with the Division by wireless, and several hundred messages were
        sent without delay.
                Pack ponies were used during the earlier stages
        to transport the ~~wireless sets~~ B.F. sets at the Brigade HQs,
        but latterly all these animals became casualties, and,
        owing to losses among the Divisional sections, could not
        be replaced .   In most cases, however, a limbered
        wagon was sent from HQ Section to move Brigade stations.
            (b). Power buzzers and amplifiers were used with
        success from the 13th to the 16th from left Brigade HQs
        at IWUY to Battalion HQs. After this, distances proved
        too great, and these instruments, although they are re-
        liable and easily get into touch with each other, suffer
        from jamming from earth return circuits, and are really
        legacies from trench warfare. They proved, however,
        valuable during the heavy shelling of IWUY.
            (c). Loop Sets were throughout used with success
        between the Brigade HQs and Brigade Communication Centres
        or Battalion HQs. Two rear sets were usually employed
        to work to each other, and a range of 6000 yards was obtained.
        Messages came through expeditiously, and little jamming
        was experienced. The Brigade Pool of Signallers have now
        confidence in these sets, and can be relied on to obtain
        touch quickly, and deal with all traffic given them, without
        delay.   Enciphering was done by Signal personnel, but a
        considerable number of messages, which gave no information
        to the enemy, was sent in clear.
            (d) C.W. stations were used for the first time by
        the Artillery in moving warfare. Communication was main-
        tained between D.A. HQ and Group HQs, but, owing to faults
        in the stations and the comparative lack of training of the
        personnel employed, working to O.Ps was precarious. A
        station in the water-tower at the Chateau at AVESNES LE SEC
        was, however, in touch with Group and D.A HQs during the
        17th and 18th October.   as
                The same difficulties/were met with in 1917 with
        Spark Wireless are at present being experienced with C.W.
        Wireless, but better instruments are now being issued, and
        the Artillery personnel, once it reaches the standard of the
        Divisional and Infantry Brigade Wireless Sections, will
        certainly repay the trouble required to train it. A good
        deal was learnt technically during these operations, and
        the comparative failure to ensure good C.W. communication
        does not affect the certainty that great use can, and will,
        be made soon of Artillery wireless.
            (e). The Divisional charging plant was adequate to
        maintain the supply of accumulators, and all stations were
        throughout provided with requisite batteries, which were
        forwarded regularly from D.H.Q.

VIII   The condition of the roads rendered motor-cycles almost
        useless for a considerable period, and mounted despatch riders
        were used. If further operations occur this winter addition-
        al mounted men will be necessary for communication between
        D.H.Q. and Brigades, and C.R.A. and Artillery Groups. There
        are only 4 D.R. horses on the establishment of the Signal
        Company H.Qs, and no assistance can be obtained from the
        cable sections, as mounted linemen are also required by them.
        The Signal Officers' chargers were used, but as Signal Officers
        require horses urgently on many occasions, this is a pre-
        carious source of supply.

IX The grouping of Brigade and Group H.Qs close to each other greatly facilitated communication. It is important, from the point of view of communications, that D.H.Q. should move in large bounds as was done in these operations. Each move of D.H.Q. necessitates a disproportionate expenditure of cable in local telephone circuits, and the diversion of, at least, half of the Divisional Sections from work on the main routes, and intermediate positions of H.Qs, are a great waste of labour and material.

                                            J.Muirhead.
                                                 Major R.E.

3/11/18.   O.C. 51st (H).Divisional Signal Co.

9841

Confidential
_____

WAR DIARY
of
51st (H) Div. Signal Co., R.E.
from 1st to 30th November, 1918.

51st H/Div. SIGNAL COY. RET. NOVEMBER 1916.

Army Form C. 2118.

WAR DIARY
or
INTELLIGENCE SUMMARY.
(Erase heading not required.)

SHEET ONE

Instructions regarding War Diaries and Intelligence Summaries are contained in F. S. Regs., Part II. and the Staff Manual respectively. Title pages will be prepared in manuscript.

Place	Date	Hour	Summary of Events and Information	Remarks and references to Appendices
IVUY	1/11/18		Cleaning up & checking stores	
	2/11/18		do.	
	3/11/18		do.	
	to 5/11/18		do	
	6/11/18		Major MUIRHEAD. D.S.O. M.C. proceeds on 1 month leave to England, Capt. ALLCARD temporarily in command of the company. No training possible as yet, owing to large numbers of men on leave.	
	7/11/18		Cleaning up billets and wagons	
	to 9/11/18			
	10/11/18	20.10	Div. Artly. move to SAULTAIN	
			Heard from 2/2 Corps Wireless that enemy were accepting Armistice terms	
	11/11/18	11.00	Hostilities ceased. General Holiday for all ranks	
	12/11/18		Div. Battn. to STARS. LA BRUYÈRE. Still manned by C.W. 40 B & Pages	
			Laid lines into G.H.Q. advanced at meeting near the village	
	14/11/18		Div. Arty. to BEAUSIES. Signal School closed down	
	15/11/18		Inspection of horses and transport & wagons	
	16/11/18 to 23/11/18		Training Wagons & recreational training etc.	

51st (H) Div. Signal Co.
R.E.T.

November 1918.

Army Form C. 2118.

WAR DIARY
or
INTELLIGENCE SUMMARY.

Sheet 2.

(Erase heading not required.)

Place	Date	Hour	Summary of Events and Information	Remarks and references to Appendices
IWUY	19/11/18 to 27/11/18		Corps H.Q. having moved to MONS, communication to them became very bad; one telephone circuit to R.A.F. H.Q. ESTADEUVRES only provided. Finding beyond army near AUBERCHICOURT almost impossible, telegrams take 10 to 18 hours to reach Corps; 23 hours to 51 Div. Arty. No DR's from Corp or Army for three days, urgent packets sent to Corps by SDR from Division. Three moto cyclists attached to corp presently used for other purposes. After repeated representations three cyclists attached to 1st. Army VALENCIENNES. Communications improve, DC not installed working to army near RAF intercommunication.	
	28/11/18 to 30/11/18		2 DR's daily from corp army.	

Allan Capt R.E.
for O.C. 51 Div. Signal Co. R.E.

98 42

Confidential
=

War Diary
of
51st (H) Div. Signal Co. R.E.
for December, 1918.

51st (H) Div. Signal Co. R.E. December 1915

Army Form C. 2118.

WAR DIARY
or
INTELLIGENCE SUMMARY.
(Erase heading not required.)

Sheet 1.

Place	Date	Hour	Summary of Events and Information	Remarks and references to Appendices
INCHY	1st to 31st		During this month the Company remained at INCHY and only routine work and maintenance of existing lines was carried out. In anticipation of a move to the area East of MONS station permanent routes and cables near LA LOUVIÈRE were reconnoitred.	

R Allward. Capt R.E.
for OC 51 Div. Signal Co. R.E.

137th (H.) Div. Signal Co.
R E

January 1919

WAR DIARY
or
INTELLIGENCE SUMMARY.
(Erase heading not required.)

Army Form C. 2118.

Place	Date	Hour	Summary of Events and Information	Remarks and references to Appendices
WUY	1-7		Preparing to move to HOUDENG. Officers & parties sent forward under Captain Abrams to test Mc Coys, lines by taking 2 lines to XXII Corps. Main line to 57 D.A. B'dex 3rd Midhurst line to 63rd B'de. SENEFFE via Mignault to 6.R.S. BRACQUIGNIES to AGUT. 137 US to GODARVILLE via MANAGE. Cables laid new routes. 157 & 164 O/S to HOUDENG.	
HOUDENG	7-		57 Div H.Qrs. to HOUDENG, Château Bock. Laid lines circuits to ad Artillery, Villettes, Forest, Aysiere. Arrow, Cable with Kiosks to 57 D. Hy. B.A. at Chateau de la Roche. Fleury, to junction at MIRELLES. 150 B'de at SENEFFE. 63 B'de R.A.F. expected. 152 Div. H.Q.	
	20-24		During this month Company observed Clerk Serjt. Willard, L.Cpl. Simpson.	
			Munzon Major	
			D Co. 137 Sgnl Co. R.E.	

WAR DIARY
or
INTELLIGENCE SUMMARY.

Army Form C. 2118.

57th Spcl Coy RET

February 1919

WO44

Place	Date	Hour	Summary of Events and Information	Remarks and references to Appendices
HOUDENG GOEGNIES	27/2/19		During this month demobilisation of the Company was enforced in nineteen drafts. Communication by wireless also has been kept intact. Established OC's leave upto the fortieth General of 62% Spcl Coy RE. Murdoch Major O.C. 57th (H) D.W. Spcl Coy R.E.T.	

Mar 1919 51st (H) Div. Signal Coy. RE

Army Form C. 2118.

WAR DIARY
or
INTELLIGENCE SUMMARY.

(Erase heading not required.)

Place	Date	Hour	Summary of Events and Information	Remarks and references to Appendices
HOUDENG-GOEGNIES	Mar 4		Demobilization proceeding. Captain Forbes to 105th Trip. Horn. Coo horse detailed by 25th Inf. Bde div. stationery collected at Bry HQ, and checked	

J M Leather Maj RE
O.C. 51st (H) Div Signal Coy. RE

www.ingramcontent.com/pod-product-compliance
Lightning Source LLC
Chambersburg PA
CBHW080236250426
43670CB00043BA/2564